REA's Test Prep Books Are The Best!

(a sample of the <u>hundreds of letters</u> REA receives each year)

(more on next page)

D1227626

(continued from front page)

" I just wanted to thank you for helping me get a great score
on the AP U.S. History exam... Thank you for making great test preps! "
Student, Los Angeles, CA

" Your *Fundamentals of Engineering Exam* book was the absolute best
preparation I could have had for the exam, and it is one of the major
reasons I did so well and passed the FE on my first try. "
Student, Sweetwater, TN

" I used your book to prepare for the test and found that the advice and the
sample tests were highly relevant... Without using any other material, I earned
very high scores and will be going to the graduate school of my choice. "
Student, New Orleans, LA

" What I found in your book was a wealth of information sufficient to shore up
my basic skills in math and verbal... The section on analytical ability was
excellent. The practice tests were challenging and the answer explanations most
helpful. It certainly is the *Best Test Prep for the GRE*! "
Student, Pullman, WA

" I really appreciate the help from your excellent book. Please keep up
the great work. "
Student, Albuquerque, NM

" I am writing to thank you for your test preparation... your book helped me
immeasurably and I have nothing but praise for your *GRE* preparation."
Student, Benton Harbor, MI

(more on back page)

THE BEST TEST PREPARATION FOR THE

CLEP

INTRODUCTORY
SOCIOLOGY

William Egelman, Ph.D.
Chair of Sociology Department
Iona College, New Rochelle, NY

Robyn A. Goldstein Fuchs, Ph.D.
Adjunct Assistant Professor
New York University, New York, NY

Sherry Larkins
Sociology Instructor
Rutgers University, New Brunswick, NJ

Paul T. Murray, Ph.D.
Sociology Professor
Siena College, Loudonville, NY

Thomas J. Sullivan, Ph.D.
Sociology Professor
Northern Michigan University, Marquette, MI

Research & Education Association
Visit our website at
www.rea.com

Research & Education Association
61 Ethel Road West
Piscataway, New Jersey 08854
E-mail: info@rea.com

The Best Test Preparation for the
CLEP INTRODUCTORY SOCIOLOGY

Year 2007 Printing

Printed in the United States of America

Library of Congress Control Number 2003105336

International Standard Book Number 0-87891-903-1

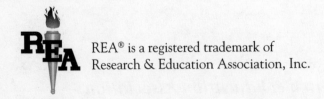

CONTENTS

CLEP INTRODUCTORY SOCIOLOGY
Independent Study Schedule

The following study schedule allows for thorough preparation for the CLEP Introductory Sociology exam. Although it is designed for six weeks, it can be reduced to a three-week course by collapsing each two-week period into one. Be sure to set aside enough time—at least two hours each day—to study. But no matter which study schedule works best for you, the more time you spend studying, the more prepared and relaxed you will feel on the day of the exam.

Week	Activity
1	Read and study Chapter 1, which will introduce you to the CLEP Introductory Sociology exam. Then take Practice Test 1 to determine your strengths and weaknesses. Score each section by using the scoring table found on page 6. You can then determine the areas in which you need to strengthen your skills.
2 & 3	Carefully read and study the Sociology Review included in this book.
4	Take Practice Test 2, and after scoring your exam, carefully review all incorrect answer explanations. If there are any types of questions or particular subjects that seem difficult to you, review those subjects by going over the appropriate section of the Sociology Review.
5	Take Practice Test 3, and after scoring your exam, carefully review all incorrect answer explanations. If there are any types of questions or particular subjects that seem difficult to you, review those subjects by going over the appropriate section of the Sociology Review.
6	Retake Practice Tests 1–3. This will help strengthen the areas where your performance is still lagging and build your overall confidence.

▼

CHAPTER 1

PASSING THE CLEP INTRODUCTORY SOCIOLOGY EXAM

Chapter 1

PASSING THE CLEP INTRODUCTORY SOCIOLOGY EXAM

ABOUT THIS BOOK

This book provides you with complete preparation for the CLEP Introductory Sociology exam. Inside you will find a concise review of the subject matter, as well as tips and strategies for test-taking. We also give you three practice tests, all based on the official CLEP Introductory Sociology exam. Our practice tests contain every type of question that you can expect to encounter on the actual exam. Following each practice test you will find an answer key with detailed explanations designed to help you more completely understand the test material.

All CLEP exams are computer-based. As you can see, the practice tests in our book are presented as paper-and-pencil exams. The content and format of the actual CLEP subject exams are faithfully mirrored. We detail the format of the CLEP Introductory Sociology exam on page 5.

ABOUT THE EXAM

Who takes the CLEP Introductory Sociology exam, and what is it used for?

CLEP (College-Level Examination Program) examinations are usually taken by people who have acquired knowledge outside the classroom and wish to bypass certain college courses and earn college credit. The CLEP is designed to reward students for learning—no matter where or how that knowledge was acquired. The CLEP is the most widely accepted credit-by-examination program in the country, with more than 2,900 colleges and universities granting credit for satisfactory scores on CLEP exams.

While most CLEP examinees are adults returning to college, many graduating high school seniors, enrolled college students, and international students also take the exams to earn college credit or to demonstrate their ability to perform at the college level. There are no prerequisites, such as age or educational status, for taking CLEP examinations. However, because policies on granting credits vary among colleges, you should contact the particular institution from which you wish to receive CLEP credit.

Most CLEP examinations include material usually covered in an undergraduate course with a similar title to that of the exam (e.g., Introductory Sociology). However, five of the exams do not deal with subject matter covered in any particular course but rather with material taken as general requirements during the first two years of college. These general exams are English Composition (with or without essay), Humanities, College Mathematics, Natural Sciences, and Social Sciences and History.

Who administers the exam?

The CLEP exams are developed by the College Board, are administered by Educational Testing Service (ETS), and involve the assistance of educators throughout the United States. The test development process is designed and implemented to ensure that the content and difficulty level of the test are appropriate.

When and where is the exam given?

The CLEP Introductory Sociology exam is administered each month throughout the year at more than 1,300 test centers in the United States and can be arranged for candidates abroad on request. To find the test center nearest you and to register for the exam, you should obtain a copy of the free booklets "CLEP Colleges" and "CLEP Information for Candidates and Registration Form." They are available at most colleges where CLEP credit is granted, or by contacting:

CLEP Services
P.O. Box 6600
Princeton, NJ 08541-6600
Phone: (800) 257-9558 (8 a.m. to 6 p.m. ET)
Fax: (609) 771-7088
Website: *www.collegeboard.com/CLEP*

Military Personnel, Veterans, and CLEP

CLEP exams are available free of charge to eligible military personnel and eligible civilian employees. The College Board has developed a paper-based version of 14 high-volume/high-pass-rate CLEP tests for DANTES Test Centers. Contact the Educational Services Officer or Navy College Education Specialist for more information. Also, visit the College Board website for details about CLEP opportunities for military personnel.

Eligible U.S. veterans can claim reimbursement for CLEP exams and administration fees pursuant to provisions of the Veterans' Benefits Improvement Act of 2004. For details on eligibility and on submitting a claim for reimbursement, visit the U.S. Department of Veterans Affairs website at *www.gibill.va.gov/pamphets/testing.htm*.

SSD Accommodations for Students with Disabilities

Many students qualify for extra time to take the CLEP Introductory Sociology, but you must make these arrangements in advance. For information, contact:

College Board Services for Students with Disabilities
PO Box 6226
Princeton, NJ 08541-6226
Phone: (609) 771-7137 Monday through Friday, 8 A.M. to 6 P.M.
    (Eastern time)
TTY: (609) 882-4118
Fax: (609) 771-7944

HOW TO USE THIS BOOK

What do I study first?

Read over the course review and the suggestions for test-taking, take the first practice test to determine your area(s) of weakness, and then go back and focus your study on those specific problems. Studying the reviews thoroughly will reinforce the basic skills you will need to do well on the exam. Make sure to take the practice tests to become familiar with the format and procedures involved with taking the actual exam.

To best utilize your study time, follow our Independent Study Schedule, which you'll find in the front of this book. The schedule is based on a six-week program, but can be condensed to three weeks if necessary by collapsing each two-week period into a single week.

FORMAT AND CONTENT OF THE CLEP

The CLEP Introductory Sociology covers the material one would find in a college-level introductory sociology class. The exam stresses basic facts and principles, as well as general theoretical approaches used by sociologists.

There are 100 multiple-choice questions, each with five possible answer choices, to be answered within 90 minutes.

The approximate breakdown of topics is as follows:

30% Social stratification (process/structure)

20% Institutions

15% Social patterns

20% Social processes

15% The sociological perspective

ABOUT OUR COURSE REVIEW

The review in this book provides you with a complete background of all the pertinent theorists, principles, and concepts of sociology. It will help reinforce the facts you have already learned while better shaping your understanding of the discipline as a whole. By using the review in conjunction with the practice tests, you should be well prepared to take the CLEP Introductory Sociology.

SCORING YOUR PRACTICE TESTS

How do I score my practice tests?

The CLEP Introductory Sociology exam is scored on a scale of 20 to 80. To score your practice tests, count up the number of correct answers. This is your total raw score. Convert your raw score to a scaled score using the conversion table on the following page. (Note: The conversion table provides only an estimate of your scaled score. Scaled scores can and do vary over time, and in no case should a sample test be taken as a precise predictor of test performance. Nonetheless, our scoring table allows you to judge your level of performance within a reasonable scoring range.)

PRACTICE-TEST RAW SCORE CONVERSION TABLE *

Raw Score	Scaled Score	Course Grade	Raw Score	Scaled Score	Course Grade
100	80	A	48	49	C
99	80	A	47	49	C
98	80	A	46	48	C
97	79	A	45	48	C
96	79	A	44	47	C
95	78	A	43	47	C
94	78	A	42	47	C
93	77	A	41	47	C
92	77	A	40	46	D
91	76	A	39	46	D
90	75	A	38	45	D
89	74	A	37	45	D
88	73	A	36	44	D
87	73	A	35	44	D
86	72	A	34	43	D
85	72	A	33	43	D
84	71	A	32	42	D
83	70	A	31	41	D
82	70	A	30	40	F
81	69	A	29	39	F
80	69	A	28	38	F
79	68	A	27	37	F
78	67	A	26	36	F
77	66	A	25	35	F
76	66	A	24	34	F
75	65	A	23	34	F
74	64	A	22	33	F
73	63	A	21	33	F
72	63	A	20	32	F
71	62	A	19	32	F
70	61	A	18	31	F
69	61	A	17	31	F
68	60	A	16	30	F
67	59	A	15	29	F
66	59	A	14	28	F
65	58	B	13	28	F
64	57	B	12	27	F
63	57	B	11	27	F
62	56	B	10	26	F
61	56	B	9	25	F
60	55	B	8	24	F
59	55	B	7	23	F
58	54	B	6	22	F
57	54	B	5	21	F
56	53	B	4	20	F
55	53	B	3	20	F
54	52	B	2	20	F
53	52	B	1	20	F
52	51	B			
51	51	B			
50	50	C			
49	50	C			

* This table is provided for scoring REA practice tests only. The American Council on Education recommends that colleges use a single across-the-board credit-granting score of 50 for all CLEP computer-based exams. Nonetheless, on account of the different skills being measured and the unique content requirements of each test, the actual number of correct answers needed to reach 50 will vary. A 50 is calibrated to equate with performance that would warrant the grade C in the corresponding introductory college course.

When will I receive my score report?

The test administrator will print out a full Candidate Score Report for you immediately upon your completion of the exam (except for CLEP English Composition with Essay). Your scores are reported only to you, unless you ask to have them sent elsewhere. If you want your scores reported to a college or other institution, you must say so when you take the examination. Since your scores are kept on file for 20 years, you can also request transcripts from Educational Testing Service at a later date.

STUDYING FOR THE CLEP

It is very important for you to choose the time and place for studying that works best for you. Some students may set aside a certain number of hours every morning, while others may choose to study at night before going to sleep. Other students may study during the day, while waiting on a line, or even while eating lunch. Only you can determine when and where your study time will be most effective. But be consistent and use your time wisely. Work out a study routine and stick to it!

When you take the practice tests, try to make your testing conditions as much like the actual test as possible. Turn your television and radio off, and sit down at a quiet table free from distraction. Make sure to time yourself. Start off by setting a timer for the time that is allotted for each section, and be sure to reset the timer for the appropriate amount of time when you start a new section.

As you complete each practice test, score your test and thoroughly review the explanations to the questions you answered incorrectly; however, do not review too much at one time. Concentrate on one problem area at a time by reviewing the question and explanation, and by studying our review until you are confident that you completely understand the material.

Keep track of your scores and mark them on the Scoring Worksheet. By doing so, you will be able to gauge your progress and discover general weaknesses in particular sections. You should carefully study the reviews that cover your areas of difficulty, as this will build your skills in those areas.

TEST-TAKING TIPS

Although you may not be familiar with computer-based standardized tests such as the CLEP Introductory Sociology, there are many ways to acquaint yourself with this type of examination and to help alleviate your test-taking anxieties. Listed below are ways to help you become accustomed to the CLEP, some of which may be applied to other standardized tests as well.

Know the format of the exam. CLEP exams are not adaptive but, rather, fixed-length tests. In a sense, this makes them kin to the familiar paper-and-pencil exam in that you have the same flexibility to go back and review your work in each section. Moreover, the format hasn't changed a great deal from the paper-and-pencil CLEP.

Read all of the possible answers. Just because you think you have found the correct response, do not automatically assume that it is the best answer. Read through each choice to be sure that you are not making a mistake by jumping to conclusions.

Use the process of elimination. Go through each answer to a question and eliminate as many of the answer choices as possible. By eliminating just two answer choices, you give yourself a better chance of getting the item correct, since there will only be three choices left from which to make your guess. Remember, your score is based only on the number of questions you answer *correctly*.

Work quickly and steadily. You will have only 90 minutes to work on 100 questions, so work quickly and steadily to avoid focusing on any one question too long. Taking the practice tests in this book will help you learn to budget your time.

Acquaint yourself with the computer screen. Familiarize yourself with the CLEP computer screen beforehand by logging on to the College Board website. Waiting until test day to see what it looks like in the pretest tutorial risks injecting needless anxiety into your testing experience. Also, familiarizing yourself with the directions and format of the exam will save you valuable time on the day of the actual test.

Be sure that your answer registers before you go to the next item. Look at the screen to see that your mouse-click causes the pointer to darken the proper oval. This takes less effort than darkening an oval on paper, but don't lull yourself into taking less care!

THE DAY OF THE EXAM

On the day of the test, you should wake up early (hopefully after a decent night's rest) and have a good breakfast. Make sure to dress comfortably, so that you are not distracted by being too hot or too cold while taking the test. Also plan to arrive at the test center early. This will allow you to collect your thoughts and relax before the test, and will also spare you the anxiety that comes with being late. As an added incentive to make sure you arrive early, keep in mind that no one will be allowed into the test session after the test has begun.

Before you leave for the test center, make sure that you have your admission form and another form of identification, which must contain a recent photograph, your name, and your signature (e.g., driver's license, student identification card, or current alien registration card). You will not be admitted to the test center if you do not have proper identification.

If you would like, you may wear a watch to the test center. However, you may not wear one that makes noise, because it may disturb the other test-takers. No dictionaries, textbooks, notebooks, briefcases, or packages will be permitted, and drinking, smoking, and eating are prohibited.

Good luck on the CLEP Introductory Sociology exam!

CHAPTER 2
SOCIOLOGY
REVIEW

Chapter 2

SOCIOLOGY REVIEW

The following sociology review covers all the major topics found in an introductory level sociology course. The review is broken down as follows:

1: **Introduction to Sociology**
2: **The Methods of Research**
3: **Socialization**
4: **Culture**
5: **Society**
6: **Social Interaction**
7: **Groups and Organizations**
8: **Deviance**
9: **Family and Society**
10: **Economics and Society**
11: **Politics and Society**
12: **Religion and Society**
13: **Social Stratification**

By thoroughly studying this course review, you will be well-prepared for the material on the CLEP Introductory Sociology exam.

1 INTRODUCTION TO SOCIOLOGY

DEFINING SOCIOLOGY

Sociology is the science or discipline that studies societies, social groups, and the relationships between people. The field encompasses both the formation and transformation of particular societies and social groups, including their continuation, dissolution, and demise, as well as the origins, structure, and functioning of social groups.

THE UNIT OF STUDY

Sociologists focus on a number of different levels of analysis in understanding social life. While some study the social interaction that occurs within groups (the social processes represented by behavior directed toward, affected by, or inspired by others in the group), other sociologists study the social structure of group life. Some are interested in the structure of societies. That is, the organization of populations living in the same area who participate in the same institutions and who share a common culture. Others in the field are concerned with the social system, a social group, or with society conceived as a whole unit distinct from the individuals that make it up.

Others concern themselves with social relationships, or relationships between people that are based upon common meaning, or with social action, defined as meaningful behavior that is oriented toward and influenced by others. But no matter what is designated to be the unit of study, the focus of the discipline is on social groups and society as a whole, rather than on the individual, which is the focus of psychology.

THE PERSPECTIVE: HUMANISTIC OR SCIENTIFIC

Some sociologists adopt a **humanistic** approach to their work, which means that they see sociology as a means to advance human welfare. They seek self-realization, the full development of a cultivated personality, or improvement of the human social condition.

On the other hand, some sociologists adopt the **scientific perspective**. They are primarily concerned with acquiring objective empirical knowledge (the actual knowledge derived from experience or observation that can be measured or counted) and not with the uses to which such knowledge is put. They believe that in science one must be concerned with "what is" and not with "what should be." Some sociologists work to integrate both humanistic and scientific perspectives.

THE SOCIOLOGICAL IMAGINATION

According to C. Wright Mills, a certain quality of mind is required if we are to understand ourselves in relation to society. This quality of mind seeks to expand the role of freedom, choice, and conscious decision in history, by means of knowledge Mills referred to as "the **sociological imagination**."

The sociological imagination expresses both an understanding that personal troubles can and often do reflect broader social issues and problems and also faith in the capacity of human beings to alter the course of human history. The sociological imagination, therefore, expresses the humanistic aspect of the sociological perspective.

THE SCIENCE OF SOCIOLOGY

As in all other sciences, the sociologist assumes there is "order" in the universe and that with methods of science the order can be understood. The sociologist, however, cannot assume that human beings will always behave in predictable ways. There are times when we do and times when we don't.

Although most of us will think and act tomorrow as we did today, some of us won't. Unlike the rocks and molecules studied by natural scientists, we are capable of changing our minds and our behavior. Unlike the organisms studied by biologists, we are capable of treating each other as whole and complete beings. Hence, the explanations and predictions offered by sociology cannot be so precise as to express universal laws that are applicable to any thing or event under all circumstances.

The Social Sciences

The social sciences are concerned with social life—psychology, with its emphasis on individual behavior and mental processes; economics, with its emphasis on the production, distribution, and consumption of goods and services; political science, with its emphasis on political philosophy and forms of government; and anthropology, with its current emphasis on both primitive and modern culture. What then distinguishes sociology from these other social sciences? In sociology the "social," however it is defined, is the immediate concern.

THE ORIGINS OF SOCIOLOGY

Compared to other academic disciplines (e.g., history, economics, and physics in particular), sociology is a discipline still in its prime. It was in 1838 that Auguste Comte coined the term from *socius* (the Latin word for "companion, with others") and *logos* (the Greek word for "study of") as a means of demarcating the field: its subject matter, society as distinct from the mere sum of individual actions, and its methods, prudent observation and impartial measurement based on the scientific method of comparison. Comte concluded that every science, beginning with astronomy and ending with sociology, follows the same regular pattern of development.

The first stage in this development is the **theological stage**. In the theological stage, scientists look toward the supernatural realm of ideas for an explanation of what they observed. In the second, or **metaphysical stage**, scientists begin to look to the real world for an explanation of what they have observed.

Finally, in the **positive stage**, which is defined as the definitive stage of all knowledge, scientists search for general ideas or laws. With such knowledge of society as how society is held together (social statics) and of how society changes (social dynamics) people can predict and, thereby, control their destiny. They can build a better and brighter future for themselves.

Was Comte's conception of a science of society ahead of its time, or was his conception of a science that would allow human beings control over lives timely? If one only considers the fast pace of technological and social change in Europe during the eighteenth century, the proliferation of factories, the spread of cities and of city life, and the loss of faith in "rule by divine right," then it would be timely. However, if one considers intellectual history, notwithstanding the accomplishments of Harriet Martineau (1802-1876) who was observing English social patterns at the same time that Comte was laying a foundation for sociology, Karl Marx (1818-1883) "the theoretical giant of communist thought" whose prophecies are still being hotly debated, and Herbert Spencer (1820-1903) whose idea that society follows a natural evolutionary progression toward something better, then Comte was clearly ahead of his time. More than 50 years passed before Emile Durkheim (1858-1917), in his statistical study of suicide, and Max Weber (1864-1920), in a series of studies in which he sought to explain the origins of capitalism, came along and tested Comte's ideas.

Under the influence of Lester Ward (1841-1913) and William Graham Sumner (1840-1910), American sociology experienced a loss of interest in the larger problems of social order and social change and began to concentrate on narrower and more specific social problems. Until 1940 attention in the discipline was focused on the University of Chicago where George Herbert Mead was originating the field of social psychology. Robert Park and Ernest Burgess were concentrating on the city and on such social problems as crime, drug addiction, prostitution, and juvenile delinquency.

By the 1940s, attention began to shift away from reforming society toward developing abstract theories of how society works and standardizing the research methods that sociologists employ. Talcott Parsons (1902-1979), the famed functionalist, touched a generation of sociologists by advocating **grand theory**. This involved the building of a theory of society based on aspects of the real world and the organization of these concepts to form a conception of society as a stable system of interrelated parts.

Robert Merton (1910-2003) proposed building middle range theories from a limited number of assumptions from which hypotheses are derived. Merton also distinguished between manifest, or intended, and latent, or unintended, consequences of existing elements of social structure which are either functional or dysfunctional to the system's relative stability. This movement succeeded despite the efforts of C. Wright Mills to reverse the trend away from activism, as well as Dennis Wrong's attempt to end the "oversocialized," or too socially determined conception of "man in sociology."

No single viewpoint or concern has dominated the thinking of sociologists since the 1970s. The questions of whether a sociologist can or should be detached and value-free, and how to deal with the individual remain controversial. Thus, sociologists have yet to agree on whether the goals of sociology are description, explanation, prediction, or control. More recently sociologists have begun to use sociological knowledge with the intent of applying it to human behavior and organizations. Such knowledge can be used to resolve a current social problem. For example, while some sociologists may study race relations and patterns of contact between minority and majority groups, applied sociologists may actually devise and implement strategies to improve race relations in the United States.

THE THEORETICAL APPROACH

Sociologists often use a theoretical approach or perspective to guide them in their work. In making certain general assumptions about social life, the perspective provides a point of view toward the study of specific social issues.

The Theory: Inductive or Deductive

A theory describes and/or explains the relationship between two or more observations. **Deductive theory** proceeds from general ideas, knowledge, or understanding of the social world from which specific hypotheses are logically deduced and tested. **Inductive theory** proceeds from concrete observations from which general conclusions are inferred through a process of reasoning.

More recent sociology includes three such approaches: **interpretative**, which includes the perspectives of symbolic interaction, dramaturgy, and ethnomethodology; **conflict theory**; and **structural functionalism**.

Interpretative Sociology

Interpretative sociology studies the processes whereby human beings attach meaning to their lives. Derived from the work of Mead and Blumer, symbolic interaction is focused on the process of social interaction and on the meanings that are constructed and reconstructed in that process. Human beings are viewed as shaping their actions based upon both the real and anticipated responses of others. Thus defined by an ongoing process of negotiation, social life is considered far from stable.

Actors are thought to be continually engaged in the process of interpreting, defining, and evaluating their own and others' actions, a process that defies explanation in lawlike terms or in terms of sociological theories proceeding deductively. Thus, out of the symbolic interactionist school of thought, the social construction of reality—the familiar notion that human beings shape their world and are shaped by social interaction—was conceived (Berger & Luckman, 1967).

Focused on the details of everyday life, the dramaturgical approach of Erving Goffman conceives social interaction as a series of episodes or human dramas in which we are more or less aware of playing roles and, thereby, engaging in impression management. We are actors seeking 1) to manipulate our audience, or control the reaction of other people in our immediate presence by presenting a certain image of ourselves; 2) to protect or hide our true selves, or who we really are offstage through "onstage," "frontstage," and "backstage" behavior; and 3) to amplify the rules of conduct that circumscribe our daily encounters.

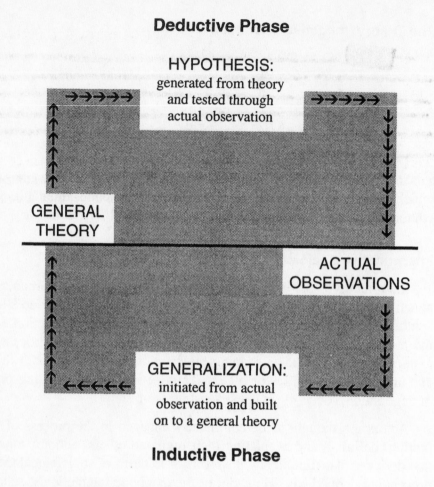

Deductive Phase

HYPOTHESIS:
generated from theory
and tested through
actual observation

GENERAL
THEORY

ACTUAL
OBSERVATIONS

GENERALIZATION:
initiated from actual
observation and built
on to a general theory

Inductive Phase

Figure 1.1 Deductive and Inductive Logical Thought

Conflict Theory

The **conflict paradigm** views society as being characterized by conflict and inequality. It is concerned with questions such as whose interests are expressed within existing social arrangements, and who benefits or suffers from such arrangements?

Sociologists viewing the social world from a conflict perspective question how factors such as race, sex, social class, and age are associated with an unequal distribution of socially valued goods and rewards (i.e., money, education, and power). Generally associated with the work of Coser, Dahrendorf, and Mills, modern conflict theory sees conflict between groups or within social organizations, and not merely class conflict (Marx), as a fact of life of any society. Conflict may have positive as well as disturbing effects (Coser). Conflict includes disagreement over who gets what, as well as tension, hostility, competition, and controversy within and between social groups over values and purposes.

Functionalism

Inspired by the writings of Emile Durkheim and Herbert Spencer, functionalism (or structural functionalism) originally took as its logical starting point a society conceived as a social system of interrelated parts, and therefore analogous to a living organism where each part contributes to the overall stability of the whole. Society, then, is seen as a complex system whose components work with one another.

The components of a society are interdependent, with each one serving a function necessary for the survival of the system as a whole. Sociologists viewing the social world from a structural-functional perspective may identify components of society and explore the functions these structures may perform for the larger system.

2 THE METHODS OF RESEARCH

DEFINING RESEARCH METHODS

The term **research methods** refers both to a strategy or plan for carrying out research and the means of carrying out the strategy. Some sociologists favor **quantitative methods**. Following the example of the natural sciences, they make use of statistical and other mathematical techniques of quantification or measurement in their efforts to describe and interpret their observations. Others favor **qualitative methods**, relying on personal observation and description of social life in order to explain behavior. Conceding that their methods entail the loss of precision, they argue that their method achieves a deeper grasp of the texture of social life. Thus, Max Weber developed the method of *verstehen*.

Verstehen is understanding as a means of characterizing and interpreting or explaining. This is done through applying reason to the external and inner context of specific social situations, such as the origins of Western capitalism.

SURVEY RESEARCH

Sociologists most often use the **survey method** of observation in their research. Subjects are asked about their opinions, beliefs, or behavior, such as how they have behaved in the past or how they intend to behave in the future, in a series of questions. The information is collected from the respondents of the survey directly by means of an interview, or indirectly by means of a self-administered written form of a questionnaire that the respondents fill out themselves. Interviews may be conducted in person, by phone, or even by electronic means of communication.

The interview may be structured where respondents are asked a series of questions in which they are given a limited choice between several possible responses on each question, unstructured where respondents are asked questions to which they can respond freely in their own words, or may involve the use of a combination of both open-ended and close-ended questions. The researcher may be interested in determining or gauging the general characteristics of a population or in collecting information about some event from the persons involved.

y **descriptive** or **explanatory**. In the latter case,
sted in understanding either causal or correla-
n variables. Variables, can either be **indepen-**
lependent variable is one that influences another
dent variable is the one being influenced by
and effect, respectively). In order to assess the
variables, controls may need to be applied. A
lifferentiating between factors that may or may
ship between variables. Relationships between
e **correlational** or **causal**. A correlational rela-
nge in one variable coincides with, but doesn't
. A causal relationship exists when a change in
es a change in the other.

research carried out? First a population is se-
be approached in the case of a relatively small
of an event that requires collecting information
hat were involved. If the population is relatively
elected for study from the entire population. A
one that accurately reflects the population from
lom sample is one where every member of the
hance of being chosen for study, as in throwing
the names of everyone in a hat, mixing them up, and selecting as many as
are thought necessary to achieve representatives. **Systematic sampling** is
a type of sample in which the nth unit in a list is selected for inclusion in
the sample. For example, every fiftieth resident listed in a phone book of a
given area will be selected. In this way, every member of the population is
guaranteed the same chance of being selected for study.

Stratified sampling uses the differences that already exist in a population, such as between males and females, as the basis for selecting a
sample. Knowing the percentage of the population that falls into a particular category, the researcher then randomly selects a number of persons to
be studied from each category in the same proportion as exists in the
population.

EXPERIMENTATION

Sociologists can and sometimes do conduct experiments. In the broadest sense, experimentation involves the observation, measurement, or
calculation of the consequences of an action. Typically the social science
researcher selects a group of subjects to be studied (the **experimental
group**), exposes them to a particular condition, and then measures the

results. The researcher usually measures the results against that of a **control group** (a similar population upon which the action has not been performed). Experiments are used to test theories and the hypotheses drawn from them. In one type of experiment, researchers create a situation in which they test the extent of the relationship that presumably exists between an independent and a dependent variable, by means of controlling a third.

Experiments may be carried out in a laboratory or in the field. Field experiments are carried out in natural settings. In one of the most famous field experiments of social science conducted in the 1930s at the Hawthorne Plant of the Western Electric Company that was located in Chicago, Elton May identified what has come to be known as the Hawthorne effect—that the mere presence of a researcher affects the subject's behavior.

OBSERVATION

Observation is a technique that provides firsthand experience of real situations. **Unobtrusive observation** is observation from a distance, without being involved in the group or activity being studied. Unobtrusive observation may be observing subjects from afar (e.g., watching children play in a schoolyard) or observing subjects more closely (e.g., watching children play in a classroom from behind a one-way mirror).

Often referred to as field research, **participant observation** is observation by a researcher who is (or appears to be) a member of the group or a participant in the activity he/she is studying. Participant observers may or may not conceal their identities as researchers. They may conceal their identities as researchers so as not to influence their subjects who, not knowing they are being observed, will act naturally. On the other hand, they may disclose their identities as researchers and seek to minimize their influence by not allowing themselves to get too involved with subjects while they are establishing a rapport.

SECONDARY ANALYSIS

Secondary analysis refers to the analysis of existing sources of information. In the hope of discovering something new, the researcher examines old records and documents, including archives and official statistics provided by the government. Thus, by using available data, the researcher avoids having to gather information from scratch, and by analyzing old records and documents, the researcher can acquire an understanding of relations between people in the past.

Content analysis refers to the techniques employed to describe the contents of the materials. They may be quantitative—using such techniques as percentages, rates, or averages to describe how the contents vary, e.g., arithmetic means, modes, or medians, or qualitative—using concepts and employing reason to capture the contents of the materials observed.

THE STAGES OF RESEARCH

Research is a process that includes:

1. Defining the problem – the questions, issues, or topic with which one is concerned.

2. Identifying and reviewing the literature or relevant literature bearing upon the problem.

3. Formulating a hypothesis – a tentative statement about what one expects to observe, e.g., the prediction of a relationship between variables or the prediction that a certain relation between people will be obtained.

4. Selecting and implementing a research design to test one's hypothesis – the plan for collecting and analyzing information.

5. Drawing a conclusion – determining whether or not one's hypothesis is confirmed and presenting one's findings in an organized way that both describes and, wherever possible, explains what one has observed.

ETHICAL PROBLEMS

Sociologists can and often do encounter ethical problems or dilemmas in conducting research. Some of the following are concerns of sociologists who conduct research:

1. What harm, if any, is the research likely to bring to participants? Does the knowledge gained justify the risks involved?

2. Is the privacy of subjects being invaded, and should the privacy of subjects be maintained under all circumstances?

3. Do subjects have a right to be informed that they are being studied? Is their consent necessary?

4. Does it matter how the research results will or can be applied?

Should this affect the research design or the way in which the research is reported?

5. When, if at all, is deception in conducting research or in reporting the research results justified?

3 SOCIALIZATION

THE PROCESS OF SOCIALIZATION AND SELF-FORMATION

Socialization is the process through which we learn or are trained to be members of society, to take part in new social situations, or to participate in social groupings. In other words, it is the prescriptive term in sociology for the process of being "social."

Generally, sociologists consider the process of socialization to be based on social interaction, the ways in which we behave toward and respond to one another. Not all sociologists agree on what is formed by such reciprocal or mutual action. Does interaction imply society, social groups, social structure, or that human beings make the perpetuation and transformation of a particular culture possible? Sociologists tend to differ in their opinion of what is learned, produced, reproduced, or altered in the process of socialization: 1) in their orientation toward society, social groups, social structure, or man-made culture; and 2) in their conception of the part, if any, human biology and individual psychology play in socialization.

Primary and Secondary Forms of Socialization

Sociologists hold the view that the individual cannot develop in the absence of the social environment—the groups within which interaction takes place and socialization occurs. Within this context, **primary socialization** refers to the initial socialization that a child receives through which he or she becomes a member of society (i.e., learns and comes to share the social heritage or culture of a society through the groups into which he or she is born). **Secondary socialization** refers to the subsequent experience of socialization into new sectors of society by an already socialized person.

Personality

Focused on society, socialization is the process through which personality is acquired, marked by the fairly consistent patterns shown in the thoughts, feelings, and activities representative of the individual. Socialization is the essential link between the individual and the social realms, without which neither is thought to be capable of surviving.

Socialization not only makes it possible for society to reproduce itself, but for society's continuity to be assured across generations as well as within generations in the personalities that are its product. This is the biological and "historical" continuity of individual and social circumstances of the life course of birth, childhood, maturity, old age, and death, and in the cultural continuity in society up to the present.

Assuming that the content of socialization varies from one person to the next as a consequence of being subject to the influence of various cultures and subcultures including race, class, region, religion, and groups in society, then every person would be different. Most of the differences would be a product of socialization, with the remainder the result of the random impact of relatively different social and cultural environments.

The socialization process is thought to explain both the similarities in personality and social behavior of the members of society and the differences that exist in society between one person and the next. It does not matter then that the two factors of nature and nurture are intimately related and cannot be separated, which is the view of most social scientists. Hence, the part that human biology plays in socialization (i.e., of nature in nurture) cannot be accurately measured. Heredity represents a basic potential, the outlines and limits of which are biologically fixed, because the socialization process is thought to be all important to the development of personality, the uniqueness, the similarities, and the differences of which are relative to society and, thereby, to the groups to which people belong.

Consistent with a view held by modern psychologists, it is argued that any instincts (unlearned, inherited behavior patterns that human beings once had) have been lost in the course of human evolution. There is no human nature outside of what culture makes of us. Hence, the concern that children raised in isolation or in institutions, who have little or no opportunity to develop the sorts of emotional ties with adults that make socialization possible, will be devoid of personality and will lack the social skills necessary to face even the simplest of life's challenges.

The process of becoming human in the sense of being able to participate in society is understood to be the process of socialization. The self at the core of personality, the individual's conscious experience of having a separate unique identity, is thought to be a social product objectively created and transformed throughout a person's life by interaction with others.

AGENTS OF SOCIALIZATION

The various agents of socialization are the individuals, groups, and institutions that supply the structure through which socialization takes place in modern societies.

Family

Generally considered the most basic social institution, the **family** is a union that is sanctioned by the state and often by a religious institution such as a church. As such, the family provides continuity in such areas as language, personality traits, religion, and class. The family is generally believed to be the most important agent of socialization in a child's social world, until schooling begins. Although the school and peer group become central to social experience as the child grows older, the family remains central throughout the entire life course.

School

As the social unit devoted to providing an education, the school provides continuity both in cognitive skills and in the indoctrination of values. Many subject areas of knowledge that may or may not be available at home, or that the modern home is ill-equipped to provide, are also provided by the school. Unlike the family, which is based on personal relationships, in school the child's social experiences broaden to include people of a variety of different social backgrounds. It is here where children learn the importance society gives to race and gender.

Peer Groups

As a primary group whose members are roughly equal in status, **peer groups** (such as play groups) provide continuity in lifestyles. Although first peer groups generally consist of a young child's neighborhood playmates, as the child meets new people at school and becomes involved in other activities, his peer group expands. It is in the peer group where the child, free of direct supervision from adults, comes to define him or herself as independent from his family. During adolescence the peer group becomes particularly important to the child and sometimes proves to be a more influential agent of socialization than the family.

Mass Media

Instrumental in making communication with large numbers of people possible, mass media provides continuity as far as knowledge or public information about the people, the events, and changes occurring in society and the threat they sometimes pose to the existing social order. Among the various kinds of mass media are books, radio, television, and motion pictures.

RESOCIALIZATION AND THE ROLE OF TOTAL INSTITUTION

Resocialization refers to the process of discarding behavioral practices and adopting new ones as part of a transition in life. For example, when one becomes a parent for the first time, he or she may have to perform new duties. Resocialization such as this occurs throughout our lives. Resocialization, however, can be a much more dramatic process, especially when it takes place in a **total institution**, such as a place of residence to where persons are confined for a period of time and cut off from the rest of society. This type of resocialization involves a fundamental break with the past to allow for the rebuilding of personality and the learning of norms and values of a new, unfamiliar social environment. The environment of a total institution is deliberately controlled in order to achieve this end. Some examples of total institutions include mental hospitals, the military, and prisons.

SIGMUND FREUD

An Austrian physician and the founder of psychoanalysis, Sigmund Freud considered biological drives to be the primary source of human activity. Activated by the pleasure principle to demand immediate and complete gratification of biological needs, the id represents these unconscious strivings without specific direction or purpose, which must be repressed and subsequently channeled in socially acceptable directions. Otherwise, without socialization the human being would be a violent, amoral, predatory animal, and organized social life would be impossible. According to Freud it is through the processes or mechanisms of identification and repression (the holding back and the hiding of one's own feelings that the human personality is formed—which is comprised of the id, the ego, and the superego. The ego represents the most conscious aspect of personality. Defining opportunities, the goals one strives toward, and what is "real," the ego controls and checks the id. Operating according to the pleasure principle, the ego deals with the world in terms of what is possible, providing limits and direction.

CHARLES HORTON COOLEY

An economist turned social psychologist, Charles Horton Cooley (1864-1924) theorized that the self-concept, which is formed in childhood, is reevaluated every time the person enters a new social situation. There are three stages in the process of self-formation, which Cooley referred to as "the **looking-glass-self**": 1) we imagine how we appear to others; 2) we wonder whether others see us in the same way as we see ourselves, and in order to find out, we observe how others react to us; and 3) we develop a conception of ourselves that is based on the judgments of others. Thus, we acquire a conception of ourselves from the "looking glass" or mirror of the reactions of others.

GEORGE HERBERT MEAD

An American philosopher and social psychologist, George Herbert Mead (1863-1931) is best known for his evolutionary social theory of the genesis of the mind and self. Mead's basic thesis—that a single act can best be understood as a segment of a larger social act or communicative transaction between two or more persons—made social psychology central to his philosophical approach. To describe the process whereby mind and self evolve through a continuous adjustment of the individual to himself and to others, Mead used several concepts: the "Me" is the image one forms of one's self from the standpoint of a "generalized others" and the "I" is the individual's reaction to a situation as he sees it from his unique standpoint.

Mead pointed out that one outcome of socialization is the ability to anticipate the reactions of others and to adjust our behavior accordingly. We do this, Mead argues, by role taking or learning to model the behavior of significant others, such as our parents. For example, playing "house" allows children to view the world from their parents' perspective.

ERVING GOFFMAN

Like other sociologists, Erving Goffman (1922-1983) considered the self to be a reflection of others—the cluster of roles or expectations of the people with whom one is involved at that point in the life course. It is the product of a series of encounters in which we manage the impression that others receive to convince others that we are who we claim to be. In every role we undertake, there is a virtual self waiting to be carried out. Goffman used the term **role-distance** to describe the gap that exists between who we are and who we portray ourselves to be.

JEAN PIAGET

Based on experiments with children playing and responding to questions, Swiss psychologist Jean Piaget (1896-1980) proposed a theory of **cognitive development** that describes the changes that occur over time in the ways children think, understand, and evaluate a situation. Piaget not only stressed the part that social life plays in becoming conscious of one's own mind, but more broadly speaking, he also observed that cognitive development does not occur automatically. A given stage of cognitive development cannot be reached unless the individual is confronted with real life experiences that foster such development. In the **sensorimotor stage**, infants are unable to differentiate themselves from their environment. They are unaware that their actions produce results, and they lack the understanding that objects exist separate from the direct and immediate experience of touching, looking, sucking, and listening.

Through sensory experience and physical contact with their environment, the infant begins to experience his surroundings differently. The world becomes a relatively stable place, no longer simply the sifting chaos it is first perceived to be. In the **preoperational stage** the child begins to use language and other symbols. Not only do they begin to attach meaning to the world, they also are able to differentiate fantasy from reality.

In the **concrete operational stage**, children make great strides in their use of logic to understand the world and how it operates. They begin to think in logical terms, to make the connection between cause and effect, and are capable of attaching meaning or significance to a particular event. Although they cannot conceive of an idea beyond the concrete situation or event, they have begun to imagine themselves in the position of another and thus to grasp a situation from the other's point of view. In effect it is during this stage of cognitive development that the foundation for engaging in more complex activities with others (such as role taking) is laid. Finally, in the **formal operational stage** the child develops the capacity for thinking in highly abstract terms of metaphors and hypotheses which may or may not be based in reality.

ERIK ERIKSON

Departing from Freud's emphasis on childhood and instinct, Erik Erikson delineated eight stages of psychosocial development in which ego identity, that sense of continuity and sameness in the conception one has of one's self that does not change over time or situation, ego development, the potential for change and growth that exists over the course of a person's life, and the social environment are involved. They are:

Stage 1—the nurturing stage, in which a child's sense of either basic trust or mistrust are established.

Stage 2—there emerges the feeling of autonomy or feelings of doubt and shame from not being able to handle the situations one encounters in life.

Stage 3—the child develops either a sense of initiative and self-confidence or feelings of guilt depending on how successful they are in exploring their environment and in dealing with their peers.

Stage 4—the focus shifts from family to school where the child develops a conception of being either industrious or inferior.

Stage 5—failure to establish a clear and firm sense of one's self results in the person's becoming confused about their identity.

Stage 6—one meets or fails to meet the challenge presented by young adulthood of forming stable relationships, the outcome being "intimacy or isolation and loneliness."

Stage 7—a person's contribution to the well-being of others through citizenship, work, and family becomes self-generative, and hence, their fulfilling of the primary tasks of mature adulthood is complete.

Stage 8—the developmental challenge posed by the knowledge that one is reaching the end is to find a sense of continuity and meaning and hence, to break the sense of isolation and self-absorption that the thought of one's impending death produces, thereby yielding to despair.

LAWRENCE KOHLBERG

Inspired by the work of Piaget to conduct a series of longitudinal and cross-cultural studies extending over several decades, Lawrence Kohlberg has concluded that given the proper experience and stimulation, children go through a sequence of six stages of moral reasoning. At the earliest stage (between ages four and ten), a child's sense of good and bad is connected with the fear of being punished for disobeying those in positions of power. During adolescence, a child's conformity to the rules is connected with the belief that the existing social order must ultimately be the right and true order and therefore ought to be followed.

Finally, there are several factors that serve as a guide to action and self-judgment among older children and young adults. These individuals have reached the highest of two stages of moral development, and are able to consider the welfare of the community, the rights of the individual, and such universal ethical principles as justice, equality, and individual dignity. Kohlberg has been criticized for basing his model of human development on the male experience, having assumed that women and girls are incapable of reaching the higher stages of moral reasoning.

CAROL GILLIGAN

Taking Kohlberg to task on this point, Carol Gilligan found that women bring a different set of values to their judgments of right and wrong. For instance, males approached the moral problem of whether or not it is wrong to steal to save a life in terms of the ethic of ultimate ends. However, females approached the same problem from the standpoint of an ethic of responsibility by wondering what the consequences of the moral decision to steal or not to steal would be for the entire family—the goal being to find the best solution for everyone involved.

In effect, these different approaches to resolving the problem can be explained by the different roles women have in our society as compared with men. Thus, Gilligan concludes there is no essential difference between the inner workings of the psyches of boys and girls.

4 CULTURE

DEFINING CULTURE

With society as the reference point, **culture** is generally defined as a blueprint according to which the members of a society or a group go about their daily lives. Culture consists of the common (learned and shared) social heritage of beliefs, customs, skills, traditions, and knowledge that members pass on to one another.

With the reference point being nothing more than individuals communicating meaning and value to one another, culture represents all things made (all objects of thought and experience), material (as in the tools we use), and nonmaterial (as in the rules people live by, the ideals according to which people live, the ideas in terms of which we think). Social structure represents the ways in which individuals have come to organize themselves internally and externally. Socialization is never complete. Deviance is very much a part of how human beings live and work as members of a community or organization.

MATERIAL AND NONMATERIAL CULTURE

Culture is comprised of material and nonmaterial elements. **Material culture** consists of the things that people attach meaning to and use. Items of material culture include cars, clothing, books, and burial sites. **Nonmaterial culture** (which includes languages, ideas, belief systems, rules, customs, political systems) consists of the abstract terms that human beings create for the purposes of defining, describing, explaining, clarifying, ordering, organizing, and communicating what they do and how they live.

In this context a symbol does not merely refer to "the representation of one thing by another." Many primates can be conditioned to make certain associations or to learn what certain verbal cues mean, but only human beings create symbols. A **symbol** represents something to which a certain meaning or value is attached by the person or persons who use it. All human languages therefore represent complex symbol systems through which thoughts are expressed but not determined. Culture includes the tools we use, the rules we live by, the ideals to which we are committed, and the ideas that we express.

ASPECTS OF CULTURE

Culture, thus, includes the symbols, sounds, events, and objects to which people attach meaning and significance.

Symbols and Language

Unlike other animals, man alone is capable of making sense of what he sees around him by using symbols to organize and communicate his observations. The one form of communication that is unique to human beings is spoken language. Human language is unlike the various types of communications used by other species that make use of symbols such as sounds, smells, and body gestures.

Norms and Values

Norms are the rules or expectations that govern or to which people orient their behavior. In this context, norms are binding rules whose violation results in some form of punishment.

Values represent not only the things that give meaning and about which human beings feel certain, but also the ideas that make such things so important that humans are willing to fight, to work, or to give up something of their own in exchange (or as payment) for them.

Values express the ideas or central beliefs common to the members of a group describing what they consider good, right, and desirable and against which the norms of a particular group or subgroup may be judged.

Folkways

Folkways are the usual customs and conventions of everyday life. Members of a society or group generally expect each other to conform to folkways, but do not insist upon such conformity. Nonconformists are thought to be peculiar or eccentric, particularly if they consistently violate such norms. Folkways differ from values in that they lack a moral component.

Mores

Mores are norms of such moral and ethical significance to the members of a society or community that their violation is regarded as a serious matter worthy of strong criticism, anger, punishment, or institutionalization.

Cultural Universals

Cultural universals are the basic elements essential to individual and collective survival that are found to exist in all cultures.

Cultural Variability

Cultural variability connotes the variety of things human beings have devised to meet their needs.

CULTURAL DIVERSITY

Ethnocentrism refers not only to the attitude that one's own cultural or ethnic values are the only good and true values, but also to the tendency to judge other cultures by one's own standards. **Cultural relativism** refers to social scientists' efforts to be objective in their observations either by not imposing their own meaning on the events being observed, or by focusing solely on the reason why the element exists.

SUBCULTURES AND COUNTERCULTURES

In today's world, cultures generally represent nations or nation-states, each with its own cultural identity. Nations, however, tend to consist of relatively large **subcultures** which, though not wholly separate from the larger culture, represent unique cultures and cultural organizations unto themselves. The Amish are one example of a subculture that has been able to preserve its traditional mode of organizing work within farming communities despite America's high level of industrialization.

All cultures are concerned with the issue of preserving their values, beliefs, language, and lifestyles and, thus, with the threat **countercultures** (whose values, beliefs, and ways of life do not conform to the norm) pose to their existence and survival. Distinctive values and norms, as well as unconventional behavior, may characterize a counterculture. Examples of countercultures include the Ku Klux Klan and other white supremacist groups, as well as cults.

5 SOCIETY

DEFINING SOCIETY

In the broadest sense possible, **society** refers to human association, i.e., to the presence of a connecting link between human beings. In that sense, any number of people interacting in ways that form a pattern or any social relationship on the basis of common meaning(s) would constitute a "society." More narrowly defined, a society is a relatively permanent grouping of people living in the same geographic area who are economically self-sufficient, politically independent, and who share a common culture.

SOCIOCULTURAL EVOLUTION

From the standpoint of society as a system, the concept of **sociocultural evolution** refers to the tendency for society (like other living organisms) to become more complex over time.

TYPES OF SOCIETIES

The ecological approach, which focuses on how much variation in cultural and social elements of the system can be attributed to the environment, provides the foundation for classifying societies.

Hunting and Gathering

Hunting and gathering societies, whose economies are based on hunting animals and gathering vegetation, have largely disappeared, with the exception of a few tribes in Africa and Malaysia. Most of these societies are nomadic in that as animal and vegetation sources are depleted, they must move in pursuit of food.

Horticultural and Pastoral

Horticultural and pastoral societies are characterized by the domestication of animals and the use of hand tools to cultivate plants. With the use of a hoe and other digging materials such as sticks, groups were able to gather their food source from one area. In places where crops were difficult to grow, domesticated animals were more often used. Material surplus develop among some horticultural and pastoral societies due to the fact that the work of a few could support many. People could produce more than they could use.

Agricultural

Agricultural societies are more complex than horticultural and pastoral societies in the level of technology used to support crops and livestock. With the advent of irrigation and the use of draft animals, farmers could produce a large surplus.

Industrial

In **industrial societies**, complex machinery and energy sources (rather than humans and other animals) are used for production. During this period evolved the use of automobiles, trains, and electronic communication such as radios, telephones, and televisions.

Postindustrial

Unlike industrial societies where the primary form of production centers around machine-generated material goods, in **postindustrial societies** information is created, processed, and stored.

THEORIES OF SOCIETY

Karl Marx, Emile Durkheim, and Max Weber all approached the concept of society from varying perspectives with concentrations on division of labor, class struggles, sociological order, biological needs and industrial and religious differences, each social theorist provided new avenues of thought for students of sociology.

Karl Marx—on History, Class Struggles, and Alienation

The German philosopher and social theorist Karl Marx (1818-1883) believed that all of human history and society can be traced to the basic material circumstance of men and women in a productive relationship with nature. Originally, wholly communal beings engaged in producing the means of subsistence as members of a tribe or family. Human beings were seen as naturally dividing their labor.

In the simplest type of society, the division of labor, however wide, is minimal, based on the different productive roles (or relations with nature) of the different sexes. With the occupational specialization accompanying the division of labor comes the capacity to produce a surplus beyond that which is necessary to satisfy basic human needs. The production of a surplus allows for the exchange of goods, a situation in which human beings become increasingly individualized. Thus, communal property is replaced by private property in the means of production.

With that, classes and class struggles emerge, and the class struggle characterizing "the history of all hitherto existing societies" begins to take its course. When the class system became so simplified as to leave only two classes (capitalist owners and working proletariat) left to fight it out, Marx predicted that this would soon end in a successful worker's revolution that would eliminate private property.

Thus, although Marx himself never completely defined the term **class**, his use of the term suggests not only a group of people who have in common a certain relationship to the means of production, but also an organization of society based on class relations that link the economic relations of production to all other relations of society.

Emile Durkheim—On Social Facts and Human Nature

French sociologist Emile Durkheim (1858-1917) laid the foundation of what has become one of the leading approaches to American sociology today by demanding a separate existence for the science of sociology on the grounds that it has both an object and a substratum exclusively its own. The object is social facts, that is, patterned regularities known through statistics to describe the collectivity as distinct from the individuals of which it is composed. The substratum is none other than society as a whole.

The logical starting point for comprehending Durkheim's conception of society is the problem of order. Durkheim believed that if one could conceive of man in a state of nature, there would be no restraints upon his aspirations, no limits on his insatiable desires, and therefore no possibility of a moral life. Thus, without the framework of a body of rules regulating interactions, conflict would be inevitable.

Durkheim concluded not only that man in a state of nature is different from other animals in that he is not satiated once his biological needs are met, but also that man in a state of nature is like other animals because his life has no meaning, rationale, or purpose outside of itself. Thus, Durkheim argued that the source of both moral life and mental life is society in the way that it sufficiently limits our insatiable desires and gives meaning to our lives.

The structure of society solidifies, and the process of society integrates most within its orbit into the whole. For instance, Durkheim reasoned that Protestantism was a less strongly integrated church than that of Catholicism because it permitted the individual greater freedom of thought and judgment and had "fewer common beliefs and practices." Durkheim attributed religious ideas concerning the ultimate meaning of life to the collective group or societal experience.

Max Weber—On Verstehen, the Ideal Type, and Rationalization

German sociologist Max Weber (1864-1920) conducted a series of investigations of culture in China, India, Greece, Rome, the Middle East, and the West in an attempt to explain why certain phenomena are unique to Western civilization. Why, for instance, did the Industrial Revolution originate in Great Britain and not, as one might expect, in China which "was already a country of large walled cities in times prehistoric by our conception"?

Deliberately stressing the factors that distinguish a particular culture from Western civilization, Weber applied the methods of **verstehen**, or understanding, to arrive at a causal explanation of the fact that in the universal history of culture no other civilization entered the path of rationalization peculiar to the West.

Weber not only made use of the ideal type concepts he developed for the purpose of arriving at such an explanation, he also applied reason and, wherever necessary, made use of the uncertain procedure of the imaginary experiment (of thinking away elements in a causal chain of motivation). He found that the Protestant ethic, the sacred value placed on all work in this world as a calling set by God, as well as saving and investment as further concrete proof of salvation, to be decisive in producing the spirit of the modern form of industrial capitalism.

In effect, Weber had determined that understanding may be of two sorts: 1) the immediate comprehension of an act or an idea one has observed, e.g., as in our direct grasp of the statement 1 + 1 + 2, and 2) the comprehension of the meaning underlying an action by intellectually grasping the sequence of motivation within the social context of shared meanings of the action.

6 SOCIAL INTERACTION

DEFINING SOCIAL INTERACTION

Consistent with Weber's view of society, every culture has a structure that can be described and analyzed. This structure represents the multitude of shared values, shared beliefs, and common expectations of a particular culture around which people have organized their lives, and leads to a certain degree of predictability in human affairs.

SOCIAL STRUCTURE, SOCIETY, AND SOCIAL SYSTEMS

Consistent with a view of society as a continuing number of people living in the same region in a relatively permanent unit, **social structure** is the way in which people's relations in society are arranged to form a network. These networks are relatively organized in the sense that there is thought to be some degree of structure and system to the patterns of social interaction of which any society is composed.

Contrary then to the latter definition, "society" here does not represent a whole. The structure is thought to be composed of similar elements of statuses (position in a society or in a group), roles (the behavior of a person occupying a particular position), groups (a number of people interacting with one another in ways that form a pattern and who are united by the feeling of being bound together and by "a consciousness of kind"), and institutions (organized systems of social relationships that emerge in response to the basic problems or needs of every society).

In terms of society constituting more than one system, social structure consists of the patterns of interaction formed by the enactment of culture (the map for living in a society). The social structure is thought to be composed of multiple systems or institutions—each considered a total system unto itself—in addition to several other types of components. It is argued that there are certain elements that are necessary to both individual and collective survival. When these elements become organized into institutional spheres, they form a society's economic system, political structure, family system, educational processes, and belief system.

Besides being determined by the social context of statuses and roles, behavior is also thought to be largely determined by the definition of the situation (the process whereby we define, explain, and evaluate the social context of the situation we find ourselves in before deciding the behavior and attitudes that are appropriate). Each system forms an arrangement or structure of statuses and roles existing apart from their occupants.

STATUS

Status may refer to a position in society and/or in a group.

Ascribed Status

An **ascribed status** is automatically conferred on a person with no effort made or no choice involved on their part such as race or sex. An ascribed status is involuntarily assumed—for example, being American Indian, a son, or a widower.

Achieved Status

The opposite status, one that is assumed largely through one's own doings or efforts, is referred to as **achieved status**. Examples of achieved statuses include being a husband, a rock star, an "A" student, and an engineering major.

Master Status

Master status is the status with which a person is most identified. It is the most important status that a person holds, not only because it affects almost every aspect of the person's life, but also because of its general symbolic value. People take for granted that a person holding the position possesses other traits associated with it.

Status Set

Status set consists of all the statuses that a person occupies. All of us occupy a number of statuses simultaneously. A woman may be a mother to her children, a wife to her husband, a professor to her students, and a colleague to her co-workers. The statuses of mother, wife, professor, and colleague together form the status set of this woman.

ROLES

Role refers to what a person does (i.e., the part they play or how one is expected to behave) by virtue of occupying a particular status or position.

Every status and role is accompanied by a set of norms or role expectations describing behavioral expectations, or the limits of what people occupying the position are expected to do and of how they are expected to do it. There are thought to be marked differences and, thus, extensive variations in how a particular role is played out, depending on differences in how those holding a particular position define their role. In effect, group differences and the conflicts they generate are thought to continually transform the system and structure.

Role Strain

Role strain refers to the situation where different and conflicting expectations exist with regard to a particular status. For example, a professor may enjoy his students and may socialize outside of class with them. At the same time, though, he is responsible for ascertaining that their performance is up to par and that they attend class regularly. To achieve this end, he may have to distance himself from his students.

Role Conflict

Role conflict occurs when a person occupies multiple statuses that contradict one another. For example, a single mother, who is the primary breadwinner, who plays on her church's softball team, and who is the den mother to her son's boy scout troop, may have conflicting roles corresponding to many of these statuses. This single mother may find that her volunteering duties conflict with her parenting and breadwinning duties.

7 GROUPS AND ORGANIZATIONS

SOCIAL GROUPS AND RELATIONSHIPS

Strictly speaking, a **group** is an assembly of people or things. However, not all people who are assembled together are thought to constitute human or social groupings. The members of a group are considered united generally through interaction, more specifically by the relationships they share, or in particular by the quality or specific character of the relationship between the individuals of which it is composed. In theory, any specific group represents no more than a relationship of "individual" persons.

ASSOCIATIONS AND COMMUNAL RELATIONSHIPS

An **association** is a type of relationship formed on the basis of an accommodation of interests or on the basis of an agreement. In either case, the basis of the rational judgment of common interest or of agreement is ultimate value or practical wisdom. A **communal relationship** is one formed on the basis of a subjective feeling of the parties "that they belong together" whether the feeling is personal or is linked with tradition. In practice, however, most actual associations and communities incorporate aspects of both types of relationships.

SOCIAL GROUPS

There are various types of social groups, from formally structured organizations to those that happen by chance. Sociologists have always been interested in types of social groups and the overall and individual characteristics of their members.

Peer Group

A peer group may be defined "as an association of self-selected equals" formed around common interests, sensibilities, preferences, and beliefs. By offering members friendship, a sense of belonging, and acceptance, peer groups compete with the family for the loyalty of their members. Peer groups serve to segregate their members from others on the basis of their age, sex, or generation. A peer group, as a type of social group, therefore consists of those whose ages, interests, and social positions or statuses are relatively equivalent and who are closely associated with one another.

Family

By contrast the family serves to emotionally bind members of all ages, sexes, and various generations. As such, the family is plagued by issues surrounding succession. Particularly in a vacillating period of social change, the conflict between the family and peer group becomes more pronounced, caused by the widening of the cultural gap that separates different generations who may even speak a different language. For example, urbanism (which allowed for sustained contact between age-mates), paved the way not only toward age-grading (the sensitivity toward chronological age gradations characteristic of modern culture), but also toward the age-graded sociability that is characteristic of our times.

Aggregates and Social Categories

Unlike an **aggregate**, which consists of a number of people who happen to be in the same place at the same time, or a **social category**, which consists of a number of people with certain characteristics in common, a **social group** consists of a collection of people interacting with one another in an orderly fashion.

In a social group, there is an interdependence among the various members which forges a feeling of belonging and a sense that the behavior of each person is relevant to each other. Thus, whether or not the membership of a social group is stable or changing, all such group relationships are thought to have two elements in common: 1) members are mutually aware of one another, and 2) members are mutually responsive to one another, with actions therefore determined by or shaped in the group context.

Social groups have been classified in many different ways—according to the group's size; nature of the interaction or the kind (quality) of the relationship that exists; whether or not membership is voluntary; whether or not a person belongs to and identifies with the group; or according to the group's purpose or composition.

Primary and Secondary Groups

Charles Horton Cooley (1864-1924) distinguished between primary groups and secondary groups. In a **primary group**, the interaction is direct, the common bonds are close and intimate, and the relationships among members is warm, intimate, and personal. In **secondary groups**, the interaction is anonymous, the bonds are impersonal, the duration of time of the group is short, and where the relationships involve few emotional ties.

CHARACTERISTICS OF GROUPS

Through the years, sociologists have developed various theories about groups. The following sections offer a sampling of these theories.

Gemeinschaft and Gesellschaft

Ferdinand Tonnies (1853-1936) distinguished between *gemeinschaft* (community) and *gesellschaft* (society). By **gemeinschaft**, Tonnies was referring to those small communities characterized by tradition and united by the belief in common ancestry or by geographic proximity in relationships largely of the primary group sort. **Gesellschaft** refers to contractual relationships of a voluntary nature of limited duration and quality, based on rational self-interest, and formed for the explicit purpose of achieving a particular goal.

Dyad and Triad

Focused on discovering the various and relatively stable forms of social relationship within which interaction takes place, George Simmel (1858-1918) made the distinction between the **dyad** of two people in which either member's departure destroys the group, and the **triad** of three, the addition of a third person sometimes serving as a mediator or nonpartisan party. An example of a triad with a mediator to close the circle is parents who strengthen their mutual love and union by conceiving a child. A nonpartisan-based triad is typified by a mediator who seeks harmony among colliding parties or who, as an arbitrator, seeks to balance competing claims.

Group Size and Other General Structural Properties

Small groups, as the name suggests, have so few members as to allow them to relate as whole persons. The smallest group consists only of two persons. Robert Bales developed the technique of **interaction process analysis**, that is, a technique of observing and immediately classifying in predetermined ways the ongoing activity in small groups.

Also, J. L. Moreno developed the technique of **sociometry**, a technique focused on establishing the direction of the interaction in small groups. An example of this technique is assessing who is interacting with whom by asking such questions as "Who is your best friend in the group?" or "Who would you most like to work with on an important project?"

In addition to size, some of the other general structural properties and related social processes affecting the functioning of social groups are 1) the extent of association (for instance, it has been suggested that the more people associate, the more common values and norms they share and the greater the tendency to get along) and 2) the social network of persons that together comprises all the relationships in which they are involved and groups to which they belong.

Interaction Processes

Also involved in the interaction processes (the ways role partners agree on goals, negotiate reaching them, and distribute resources) are such factors as:

1) the differentiation between the characteristics of the role structure with task or instrumental roles. Instrumental roles are "oriented toward specific goals and expressive roles, which are instrumental in expressing and releasing group tension.

2) front stage (public) and backstage (free of public scrutiny) behavior.

3) principles of exchange (characteristic of market relationships in which people bargain for the goods and services they desire).

4) competition between individuals and groups over scarce resources in which the parties not only agree to adhere to certain rules of the game but also believe they are necessary or fair.

5) cooperation (an agreement to share resources for the purpose of achieving a common goal).

6) compromise (an agreement to relinquish certain claims in the interest of achieving more modest goals).

7) conflict (the attempt by one party to destroy, undermine, or harm another) and such related methods of reducing or temporarily eliminating conflict as coaptation (the case of dissenters being absorbed into the dominant group), mediation (the effort to resolve a conflict through the use of a third party), and the ritualized release of hostility under carefully controlled circumstances such as the Olympics games.

In-Group and Out-Group

Other types of social groups include **in-groups** which, unlike **out-groups** (those groups toward which a person feels a sense of competition or opposition), are those to which "we" belong.

Reference Group

Reference groups are social groups that provide the standards in terms of which we evaluate ourselves. For example, if a college student is worried about how her family will react to her grades, she is using her family as a reference group. Similarly, if a lawyer is worried about how the other partners of his firm will react to a recent case he lost, the lawyer is using his colleagues as a reference group.

Group Conformity and Groupthink

Research on groups has illustrated the power of group pressure to shape human behavior. **Group conformity** refers to individuals' compliance with group goals, in spite of the fact that group goals may be in conflict with individual goals. In an attempt to be accepted or "fit in," individuals may engage in behaviors they normally would not.

Groupthink, a related phenomenon, occurs when group members begin to think similarly and conform to one another's views. The danger in this is that decisions may be made from a narrow view. Rather than exploring various sides of an issue, group members seeking conformity may adopt a limited view.

GROUP LEADERSHIP

Leadership is an element of all groups. A leader is a person who initiates the behavior of others by directing, organizing, influencing, or controlling what members do and how they think.

Instrumental and Expressive Leaders

Group research has found two different types of leaders: instrumental (task-oriented leaders who organize the group in the pursuit of its goals) and expressive (social-emotional leaders who achieve harmony and solidarity among group members by offering emotional support).

Authoritarian, Democratic, and Laissez-faire Styles of Leadership

Among the various styles of leadership are the authoritarian leader who gives orders, the democratic leader who seeks a consensus on the course of action to be taken, and the laissez-faire leader who mainly lets the group be—doing little if anything to provide direction or organization.

ORGANIZATIONS

In the sense in which sociologists use the term, an **organization** represents a specific type of social relationship or arrangement between persons that is either closed to outsiders or that limits their admission. Regulations are enforced by a person or by a number of persons in authority active in enforcing the order governing the organization.

Formal Organization

In the latter sense, a **formal organization**, which represents a type of group or structural pattern within which behavior is carried out in a society, is characterized by 1) formality, 2) a hierarchy of ranked positions, 3) large size, 4) a rather complex division of labor, and 5) continuity beyond its membership.

BUREAUCRACY

A **bureaucracy** is a rationally designed organizational model whose goal it is to perform complex tasks as efficiently as possible.

Weber's Ideal Type

The basic organization of society may be found in its **characteristic institution**. In prehistoric times, the characteristic institution of most societies was the kin, clan, or sib. In modern times, particularly in the West, as cities became urban centers for trade and commerce, the characteristic institution became, and remains today, a bureaucracy.

A bureaucracy is a rational system of organization, administration, discipline, and control. Ideally, a bureaucracy has the following characteristics:

1) Paid officials on a fixed salary which is their primary source of income.

2) Officials who are accorded certain rights and privileges as a result of making a career out of holding office.

3) Regular salary increases, seniority rights, and promotions upon passing exams.

4) Officials who qualify to enter the organization by having advanced education or vocational training.

5) The rights, responsibilities, obligations, privileges, and work procedures of these officials are rigidly and formally defined by the organization.

6) Officials are responsible for meeting the obligations of the office and for keeping the funds and files of that office separate from their personal ones.

Bureaucracy in Real Life

Weber never meant for his ideal type conception of bureaucracy to be confused with reality. Rather he intended that it be used as a measuring rod against which to measure empirical reality (as grounded in perceived experience). In so doing Joseph Bensman and Bernard Rosenberg (1976) learned, for instance, that most modern bureaucrats are "people pushing" rather than "pencil pushing" types of white collar employees. The advancement opportunities for these employees hinge as much on how well they are liked, trusted, and how easy they are to get along with as on how well they objectively qualify for a position.

Once alert to the cash value in terms of income-producing opportunities of having "personality" in an employee society, the official begins to see him/herself as a salable item to be marketed and packaged like all other merchandise.

Such a self-rationalization as described by Karl Mannheim (1940) shows systematic control of impulses as a first step in planning one's course in life. In accordance with the official's goals, he compares his assets, liabilities, and background to what the market will bear as a first step in the research process of determining how his personality must be altered to meet the market's fluctuating demand.

Although the standards one must conform to will vary from one organization to the next, bureaucrats share the inclination to look for external standards upon which to base one's interests, activities, and thoughts. Thus, the appearance of a warm and friendly atmosphere belies the reality of the tensions that exist but that cannot be aired in public. As a compromise, occasions where spontaneity and controlled warmth are deemed acceptable are planned.

In these ways, officials never really internalize their roles or parts. They have no commitment to the organization or to one another beyond the formal requirements of their positions. The bureaucrat's all-too-human quest for personal identification (to personally identify with and relate to people on genuine terms) makes true bureaucratic impersonality impossible to achieve.

Parkinson's Law

In this context, we can begin to understand two well-known criticisms of bureaucracy expressed in **Parkinson's Law**. Named after its author, C. Northcote Parkinson, Parkinson's Law states that in any bureaucratic organization "work expands to fill the time available for its completion."

The Peter Principle

Named after Lawrence Peter, the **Peter Principle** states that "in any hierarchy every employee tends to rise to his level of incompetence."

Michels' Iron Law of Oligarchy

We can now also begin to understand the context within which Robert Michels formulated his famous **Iron Law of Oligarchy**. As observed by Bensman and Rosenberg, the speedy proliferation of bureaucracy "is connected with everything else that gives our culture its uniqueness," i.e., a money economy, machine production, and the creation of nation-states with large-scale bureaucratized armies.

Bureaucracy, according to Michels, also spreads throughout the various branches of civil government following the widening of the political boundaries of the territory under the control of a single person. When workers organized for the purpose of protecting and of advancing their claims to having certain inalienable rights (whether, say, to form trade unions or political parties), their leadership is bureaucratized.

Thus, Michels, cognizant of the significance of working-class movements in America and in Europe when he drafted the Iron Law of Oligarchy, believed that a small number of specialists generally hold sway over any organization.

8 DEVIANCE

DEFINING DEVIANCE

Strictly speaking, **deviance** represents a departure from a norm. Although deviance is usually associated with criminal activity or mental illness, it also includes behavior that stands out as being more ambitious, industrious, heroic, or righteous than the rest—behavior which is generally not expected nor very frequently found.

However, sociologists have primarily concerned themselves with deviant behavior that violates or is contrary to the rules of acceptable and appropriate behavior of a group or society. This becomes evident in the strong negative reaction, or ridicule, generated by the members of the group.

Sociologists have tended to differ in their understanding of deviance. The question is whether or not deviance represents more than a violation of a norm and, if so, what this contrary behavior is thought to ultimately represent.

DEVIANCE AND STIGMA

Consistent with an orientation toward society as a whole, the one characteristic shared by those with a deviant reputation is stigma. A **stigma** is the mark of social disgrace that sets the deviant apart from other members of society who regard themselves as "normal." In most instances, people escape having their deviant behavior discovered. Because they are not stigmatized or marked deviant, they think of themselves as being relatively normal.

Deviance is seen as relative to the time, place, and context of a group or society in which it is observed. In addition, it is also relative to the social status of the person doing the defining, and to whether or not that person is in a position to label the behavior as "deviant."

CONFORMITY, SOCIAL ORDER, AND SOCIAL CONTROL

Even if most people have violated significant social norms at some point in their lives, the majority of people at any given moment are thought to be conforming to those norms that are important to a society's continued existence. It is because of this that social order exists.

It is believed that a social order depends on its members generally knowing and doing what is expected of them. They have common values and guidelines to which they generally adhere. These norms prescribe the behavior that is appropriate to a situation as it is given or commonly construed at the time. In other words, a social order presumably cannot exist without an effective system of social control. Social control is best defined as a series of measures that serve as a general guarantee of people conforming to norms.

Through the process of socialization, social control is achieved. The success of this process is demonstrated by the fact that most people usually do what is expected out of sheer habit, and without question. When socialization cannot guarantee sufficient conformity through the informal, as well as the formal and organized ways of rewarding conformity and punishing nonconformity, there becomes a need for negative sanctions. Negative sanctions indicate that social control has failed and that deviance has occurred.

Deviance represents a residual category of behavior unlike that which is generally found. This behavior, unless adequately checked, may threaten the effectiveness of the system of social control and the social order. Ultimately some deviance is necessary so that the boundaries of permissible behavior may be defined. The major function of deviance is to reassure people that the system of social control is working effectively.

DEVIANCE AND SOCIAL GROUPS

Consistent with an orientation to social groups and the process through which conformity to norms is structured or organized in them, deviance represents an unusual departure from an established group rule of acceptable conduct. These norms denote a negotiated world of meanings; these are rules that shape what individuals perceive and how they behave, thereby eliminating the uncertainty that exists in the absence of such behavior guidelines. The acknowledgment of such a departure assures members that they are "normal." Members can feel that their own behavior falls within the usual parameters of what is and what is not acceptable in the group, while ridiculing those whose observed behavior departs from the expected.

In this way, the social order, which depends upon people doing what others expect of them, is more or less guaranteed. Those who usually behave in socially approved ways are provided with a reason for continuing to do what is expected and are momentarily relieved of their anxiety about the unusual occurring too soon again. Those who have departed from a norm have a reason to avoid behaving in ways that are unacceptable to group members.

Given the many different groups that make up a society, and the competing values and the diversity of interests they represent, social order is never guaranteed or certain without there being value systems. These value systems enjoy such wide acceptance in society that even those groups that represent opposing interests find them to be consistent with, or suited to, their own concerns.

In the competition or struggle between groups, those with the most to lose or gain in terms of immediate self-interest, or those who feel most strongly about their cause, may succeed in defining and shaping the standards of right and wrong that become the group's norms. But they may never succeed in altering the meaning that represents the core values or culture of a society.

As previously noted, the latter are acquired during primary socialization and are thought to be a product of unique circumstances. Thus, deviant behavior is not essentially different from that of conformity.

Both roles are socially constructed relative to the culture of the society in which they thrive. Therefore, the processes and actions that are defined as deviant in our society are merely those that fall outside the canon of processes and actions that are defined as conformist.

These "deviant" actions are those that powerful people, those in a position to both define and enforce social norms, find threatening. Because this sector of society agrees with, supports, and serves to define the status quo, anything that threatens this sector is then labeled deviant. In this way, deviance is defined by its opposite rather than any inherent threat it may pose.

Particularly in complex societies, some norms are thought to be more important than others in that they involve behavior necessary to a group's continuity, survival, or well-being. This is evidenced by the severity of the sanctions associated with them. Whether or not norms are proscriptive ("thou shalt not") or prescriptive ("thou shalt"), they all are thought to be relatively arbitrary in principle. Their definition changes over time and from one society to the next but never so much as to be inconsistent with a society's core values.

FUNCTIONS OF DEVIANCE

In terms of the group, deviance serves several functions. Consistent with Durkheim's viewpoint, deviance serves to unify the group by identifying the limits of acceptable behavior and thus identifying who are insiders and who are outsiders. Deviance also serves as a safety valve that allows people to express discontent with existing norms without threatening the social order. Principled challenges to norms are possible.

Social control refers to the ways of getting people to conform to norms. Such techniques, which include persuasion, teaching, and force, may be planned or unplanned, may be informal (involving the approval or disapproval of significant others) or formal (involving those in positions responsible for enforcing norms). In this context, **primary deviance** is the term used to refer to behavior violating a norm, while **secondary deviance** refers to the behavior that results from the social response to such deviance.

It is in connection with secondary deviance that stigma symbolizes a moral blemish or undesirable label that tends to be extended to other undesirable traits. Deviant subcultures represent peer groups that support deviance by providing social networks to deviants.

BIOLOGICAL EXPLANATIONS OF DEVIANCE

In 1875 Cesare Lombroso published the results of his work comparing the body measurements of institutionalized criminals, non-criminals, and primitive human beings. He had concluded that deviant behavior is inherited and that the body measurements of criminals bore a greater resemblance to apes than to non-criminals.

William Sheldon (1941) based his work on the earlier work of Ernst Kretschmer (1925). He classified people according to their body types. He concluded that a relationship exists between body type, psychological state, and criminal behavior (with short and fat endomorphs being prone to manic depression and alcoholism; thin and small ectomorphs being prone to schizophrenia; and muscular and large boned mesomorphs being prone to criminal behavior, alcoholism, and manic depression).

Such studies attempting to link criminal behavior and body type have not always produced consistent results. More recently efforts have been made to link deviant behavior with an "abnormal" (XYY) chromosomal pattern found among inmates of prisons and mental hospitals. This pattern is unlike the usual male XY pattern or female XX pattern. Researchers also have been studying the relationship between the brain and body chemistry, diet, and behavior.

PSYCHOLOGICAL EXPLANATIONS OF DEVIANCE

Psychologists have attributed antisocial or deviant behavior to the unconscious making itself known to a superego that lacks the strength to overcome the id. This way of thinking was influenced by Freud and others who sought to trace personality and behavior to early childhood learning experiences and the manner in which the repression of the powerful biological drives of the id takes place. The unconscious is that part of the mind where unpleasant, or perhaps even antisocial, memories of experience are stored.

Such research has supported the use of personality tests to identify troublemakers and delinquents, to assess the guilt or innocence of those suspected of committing a crime, and to ferret out problems before they occur.

SOCIOLOGICAL EXPLANATIONS OF DEVIANCE

Sociological explanations of deviance fall into two categories. The first category includes those sociologists who assume that most people conform most of the time as a consequence of adequate socialization. They treat deviance as a special category of behavior and the deviant as deserving of special consideration. They ask why every society has known deviance. They want to know why people become deviant. They wonder why social control mechanisms are applied as a means of limiting and punishing clear violations of significant social norms.

Sociologists also tend to locate the source of deviance outside the individual person. They look within the social structure or in a social process of labeling. Labeling focuses on the process through which persons come to be defined as deviant. It also focuses on the means through which deviant behavior is created through the interaction taking place between those committing acts in violation of group's norms and those responding to such violations.

Robert Merton (1957) expanded upon Durkheim's understanding of deviance as the product of a structural circumstance of disorganization in the individual and in society. Both Merton and Durkheim saw this as a result of weak, inconsistent, or even nonexistent social norms. Merton concluded that in American society, for example, there is a disjunction between means and ends, such as the emphasis on wealth and success without many legitimate means to achieve them. Those individuals without such opportunities attempt to bridge this gap in a number of ways:

- The "conformist" seeks to continue the acceptance of the goals and means offered for their attainment.

- The "innovator" may continue to accept the goals while seeking new, and in many cases, illegitimate revenues for the attainment of these goals.

- The "ritualist" may make the means into an end by rejecting the culturally prescribed goals as being out of his reach. This person is in favor of an overemphasis upon the means of achieving these goals. An example of this would be the bureaucrat who is more concerned with adhering to the rules and with keeping his job, than with his own personal achievement.

- The "retreat" rejects both the means and ends offered by society by dropping into drug use, mental illness, alcoholism, homelessness.

- The "rebellious" reject both the means and ends while seeking to replace both with alternatives, thereby changing the way society as a whole is structured.

In his theory of differential association, Edwin Sutherland (1939) concluded that criminal behavior is learned through social interaction in primary groups. His theory states that it is in the primary group where a person acquires knowledge of the techniques used in committing crimes. This primary group also provides reasons for conforming to or violating rules of permissive or not permissive behavior in a given situation, as well as an understanding of what motivates criminal activity. It is claimed that becoming a criminal means that the definitions favorably outweigh those unfavorable to violating the law. Moreover, the kinds of differential associations favoring criminal activity occur frequently, are long lasting and intense, and take place earlier rather than later in life.

9 FAMILY AND SOCIETY

FAMILY AS A BIOLOGICAL AND SOCIAL UNIT

Social institutions, including family, economy, government, and religion, are organized patterns of beliefs and behaviors focused on meeting society's basic needs. The family is a social creation that transcends the biological basis of its existence. As a unit of organization, it is of particular interest to sociologists.

KINSHIP

Kinship is the introduction of symbolic meaning or value to actual or imagined blood ties. Although the biological phenomenon of unity based on reproducing and protecting animal offspring predates man, kinship is a specifically human, intellectual creation. Max Weber found it possible to establish the social origins of kinship by means of cross-cultural comparisons.

The concept of social inheritance is the inheritance of achieved and ascribed statuses, wealth, prestige, and power transmitted to the young from the parents. It has been the focus of ideological warfare between church and state, and it has been an agent for socialization as well as of oppression.

MARRIAGE

This social institution, found in every society, is generally seen as a social group consisting of two or more people, related by marriage, blood, or adoption, who often reside together. Marriage is an enduring, legally sanctioned union that ideally involves both economic cooperation and sexual intimacy between husband and wife.

TYPES OF FAMILIES

In broadest terms, two types of families are possible. The family of orientation is the unit into which a person is born. The family of procreation is the unit, usually occurring in adulthood, when people are able to form social groups of their own through procreation or adoption.

The nuclear family consists of people of the opposite sex who are in a socially approved sexual union and living with their children. The extended family is one in which the notion of consanguinity has been extended beyond the immediate (nuclear) family to those families who are indirectly linked by blood.

FORMS OF VESTED AUTHORITY

Authority can be vested in either the father or the mother of a family. When the father is vested authority, the family is referred to as a **patriarchy**. When the mother is vested authority, the family is referred to as a **matriarchy**.

The terms **patrilineal** and **matrilineal** indicate where descent may be traced (through the father or mother).

ENDOGAMY AND EXOGAMY: MARRIAGE PATTERNS

Most societies practice **endogamy** (marriage within certain specific groups) or **exogamy** (marriage outside certain specific groups). In the United States, for instance, marriage within one's immediate family is not permitted; he or she must marry an outsider. This is known as exogamy.

However, interracial marriages are often discouraged. Hence, social pressure exists to avoid marrying someone of a different race, which in this case is considered an unacceptable form of exogamy.

MONOGAMY AND POLYGAMY: MARRIAGE PATTERNS

Monogamy means having one spouse at a time. Serial monogamy, which involves marriage, divorce, followed by remarriage, has become less of the exception and more the rule in America.

Polygamy means having more than one spouse at a time. Three types of polygamy are known to exist. The first is **polygyny**, which refers to the practice of a man having several wives at once. The second is **polyandry**, which refers to the practice of a woman having several husbands at once. The third type is **group marriage**, which refers to a marriage between two or more men and two or more women.

RESIDENTIAL PATTERNS: PATRILOCALITY, MATRILOCALITY, AND NEOLOCALITY

Patrilocality, matrilocality, and neolocality indicate where newlyweds customarily reside. **Patrilocality** occurs when the newlyweds reside with the husband's extended family; **matrilocality** occurs when they reside with the wife's extended family; **neolocality** occurs when they live in a new or separate residence.

Because there is no necessary correlation between power, descent, and residence, patriarchies may be matrilineal or matrilocal, they may include the levirate (which obliges a man to marry his brother's widow or suffer disgrace), or they may permit the transmission of property to the eldest son, a practice called primogeniture, or to the youngest son, which is called ultimogeniture.

10 ECONOMICS AND SOCIETY

TRADITIONALISM AND ECONOMIC RATIONALITY

From the standpoint of society as a whole, the economic order is the institutionalized organizational system of norms and behavioral patterns through which goods and services are produced, distributed, and consumed. By definition economic life includes the work we do, what type of economic organization we belong to, why we do it, and the measure of success attained as shown by wealth, property, income, and the occupation itself.

In this context, traditionalism represents the type of economic motivation that sanctifies the past by preserving a certain practice because it has always been that way. Its opposite, economic rationality, represents the type of economic motivation that embraces change and development, such as in the methods of production. Economic rationality sanctifies progress and emphasizes practicality, with profits being "the touchstone of economic efficiency."

In the past, guild masters had monopolized their positions of power based on a heredity, and created a class of workers who had no chance of becoming masters themselves. Changes were brought about in the methods of production and the rules governing how much capital equipment a guild master could own, and how many journeymen he could employ. These economic changes brought about the crystallization of the class comprised of capitalists and workers known as the "working class."

DIVISION OF LABOR

The **division of labor** is the manner in which work is divided among individuals and groups specialized in particular economic activities.

COMPARATIVE ECONOMIC SYSTEMS

Capitalism represents one type of economic system in which there is private ownership of the means of producing and distributing goods and services. The most widely used example of a capitalist society is the United States.

Socialism represents another type of economic system in which there is public ownership of the means of producing and distributing goods and services. Actual economic systems, however, are more often a blend of capitalist and socialist elements today. Although the former Soviet Union possessed an economy based on socialism, today the People's Republic of China is the best example of a socialist economy.

SECTORS OF THE ECONOMY

The primary, secondary and tertiary sectors of economy involve the different ways of producing goods and services and selling them for a profit.

Primary Sector

The **primary sector** is involved in the extraction of raw materials and natural resources. Primary production consists of such activities as hunting, gathering, farming, and mining in which people are involved directly with the extraction and cultivation of natural resources.

Secondary Sector

The **secondary sector** is involved in turning the raw materials acquired through primary production into the manufactured goods we use, such as furniture, cars, and homes. Secondary production involves the techniques and activities involved in manufacturing goods, i.e., in making such items as pottery, bows and arrows, cards, and nuclear weaponry.

Tertiary Sector

The **tertiary (or service) sector** is involved in providing services in such areas as health, education, welfare, and entertainment. Tertiary production consists of the kinds of assistance or service that people offer, such as baby-sitting, plumbing, keyboarding, teaching, and nursing.

DISTRIBUTION SYSTEMS

The various types of distribution systems include the barter system, which consists of the direct exchange of some goods or services for others judged to be of equivalent value. Prior to the use of money as a medium of trade, individuals bartered. For example, a woman who needs a house built may exchange some of her land for the wood necessary to build the house.

The free-market system of exchanging goods and services is one in which value is determined by supply and demand.

11 POLITICS AND SOCIETY

THE POLITICAL ORDER

From the standpoint of society as a whole, the political order is the institutionalized system of organization and behavioral patterns through which power is legitimately acquired and exercised.

As understood by Max Weber, a belief in legitimacy, the right of those in positions of power to command, is fundamental to all forms of authority. Without the consent of the governed, the state's monopoly on the legitimate use of force is more than likely to be questioned.

THREE TYPES OF AUTHORITY

Max Weber differentiated between three types of authority: traditional, rational-legal, and charismatic. He divided them according to how the right or power to command and the duty to obey are interpreted. **Traditional authority** is based on long-held and sacred customs. **Rational-legal authority** stems from within the framework of a body of laws that have been duly enacted. **Charismatic authority** is based on the extraordinary, uncanny, and supernatural powers or abilities that have been associated with a particular person.

Thus, in pre-industrial times, traditional authority, the power generated by respect for long-held norms, dominated. As societies industrialized, however, the importance of traditional authority declined. Charismatic authority exists when power is legitimated through the unique, extraordinary personal abilities of an individual. Individual leaders who are seen by the public as magnetic and forceful are granted power. Typically rational-legal authority, which is legally circumscribed by rules and regulations, is found being exercised within modern formal organizations.

TYPES OF GOVERNMENT

Forms of government depend upon the type of relationship that exists between the ruler and the ruled. The types of government are as follows: authoritarian, totalitarian, and democratic.

Authoritarian

An **authoritarian** form of government is one in which rulers tolerate little, if any, opposition to their authority. Such governments deny popular participation in decision making. Individuals have little or no voice in government operations.

Totalitarian

A **totalitarian** government is one in which there are in principle no recognizable limits to authority that rulers are willing to acknowledge. The government extends control over many aspects of citizens' lives.

Democratic

A **democratic** government is one in which authority ultimately lies with the people, whose participation in government (i.e., both in the decision-making processes as well as in the process of appointing, electing, or dismissing rulers) is considered a right.

THE POLITICAL PROCESS

A political party is an organization seeking to gain control of government through legitimate means. In the United States, where many people hold political attitudes that are both liberal and conservative, party identification is relatively weak.

Interest groups are those groups or organizations seeking to influence political decisions that may affect their members. It is a political alliance of people who are interested in some social or economic issue. Lobbyists are the advocates or the "voice" of special interest groups.

C. WRIGHT MILLS—THE POWER ELITE

In 1956 C. Wright Mills published *The Power Elite*. Looking at the social class of leaders in major areas of influence and authority (including business and government), he found that they not only share a singular vision of what is fair and good but also that they act in ways that serve their interest in maintaining the existing stratification system and, thereby, their position in it.

In Mills's terms at the highest level of power are "warlords, corporate chieftains, and the political directorate," who together and in cooperation with one another comprise America's power elite. A highly organized group of only a few people who make decisions on behalf of or for the many, the power elite consists of military leaders, politicians, and business leaders who are responsible to no one but themselves.

G. WILLIAM DOMHOFF'S GOVERNING CLASS

Attempting to learn whether or not America actually has the sort of ruling class described by Mills, G. William Domhoff studied the people listed in the Social Register, to identify those who have attended a select private school, who are millionaires, and who are members of prestigious men's clubs in large cities. He found that these people, who comprise the upper class in America, represent less than 0.5 percent of the population.

Besides being extremely wealthy, many hold high-level positions in corporations, banks, insurance companies, the CIA, government offices, the mass media, charitable organizations, and as trustees of colleges and universities. They also comprise a close-knit group of people united by intermarriage, through their educational experience of attending the same schools, as members of the same clubs, and as board members of the largest corporations.

DAVID RIESMAN'S PLURALIST VISION

Although agreeing with Mills that there is an unequal distribution of power in the United States, David Riesman (1961) rejects the notion that the power holders are, or can be, a unified group. The diversity of interests that exist in mass society makes it impossible for any single group to dominate society by controlling the decision-making process. Thus, Riesman understood the system of rule to be made up of various sectors of power, each serving as a potential buffer against any one group gaining control of the decision-making process throughout the system.

12 RELIGION AND SOCIETY

THE LINK BETWEEN RELIGION AND SOCIETY

The term **religion** means a theory, creed, or body of dogma that seeks to comprehend the universe and man's place in it, god or the gods, as well as the supernatural realm. Every religion seeks to establish a meaningful coherent image of the natural and supernatural world. For some sociologists, however, religion represents more than just a "system" or methodically organized set of beliefs. Religion constitutes a totality of commonly held beliefs and rites oriented toward the realm of the sacred or supernatural. In this sense, every religion is thought to be social in its origins and in its affects. Religion ultimately serves a cohesive function in maintaining the whole of society. Specifically, religions have been linked with:

1. Codes of ethics – Confucianism, for example, is a very practical religion that places little emphasis on the supernatural world and a great deal of emphasis on seeing a situation for what it is and then applying the rules that are appropriate to the situation.

2. Personality – Religion has been a factor in both the persecution or exaltation of certain groups, as well as the development of social mores. For these reasons, the religious climate can have a dramatic effect on the personality of an individual or community.

3. Historical condition – Religion has also fostered polarized world views that tend to have a this-worldly or an other-worldly orientation, such as medieval monasticism, which emphasized withdrawal from this world in order to prepare for eternity.

4. Theodicy – A religious explanation for what seems to be the senseless distribution of good and bad fortune that enables believers to continue to have faith under any circumstances.

The Sacred and the Profane

Sacred refers to the sphere of ideas, activities, persons, objects, abilities, and experiences that have been deemed holy, divine, supernatural, or mystical and, hence, unalterable. **Profane** refers to the visceral sphere of objects, persons, and behaviors capable of being understood and of being altered.

SOCIOLOGICAL PERSPECTIVES ON RELIGION

Durkheim

Emile Durkheim saw religion as validating the existence of society. In *The Elementary Forms of Religious Life*, Durkheim states that the collective experience of religious society not only serves as the foundation for ideas about life's ultimate meaning, but also for the ceremonies that seek to express this meaning.

Weber

Concerned about the relationship between thought and action, Max Weber studied the central tenets of Islam, Buddhism, Hinduism, Confucianism, Christianity, and Judaism to determine how each established psychological and practical grounds for economic activity. In *The Protestant Ethic and the Spirit of Capitalism*, Weber showed how the belief in predestination and in an unbridgeable gulf between man and God emphasized personal responsibility for one's own salvation. This generated anxiety regarding one's status in the afterlife that proved to be compatible with a work ethic that called for the accumulation of capital as proof of salvation.

FORMS OF RELIGIOUS ORGANIZATION— CULT, SECT, CHURCH

The simplest form of religious organization, a **cult**, consists of a small group of followers surrounding a charismatic religious leader. Unlike a cult, a **sect** does not depend on the kind of personal inspiration offered by a charismatic leader for its continuity. Typically, a **church** claims universal membership over those born into it, and they can only leave it through expulsion. This is the very opposite of a cult in that its leadership is formally established, its economic foundation has been institutionalized, membership is by birth (not voluntary), and sanctions take the form of interdiction and excommunication

WORLD RELIGIONS

World religion is understood as "a system of life regulation" capable of attracting a multitude of constituents. Thus, the religious ethics of the Confucian, the Hindu, the Buddhist, the Christian, and the Muslim belong to what Max Weber characterized as "the category of world religions."

Unlike those religions of the West and Middle East—Judaism, Christianity, and Islam—which emphasize one god (monotheism) and this-worldliness, the religions of Southeast Asia and the Far East tend not only to be oriented toward nature and the afterlife, but also to be polytheistic (emphasizing many gods). Buddhism, Hinduism, Shintoism, and Confucianism address questions related to humans' place in the universe, the path to happiness, and the meaning of life. Thus, unlike Islam, Judaism, and Christianity which stress the importance of received doctrine, these other religions stress the element of soul searching and other techniques of solving the riddle of life's ultimate meaning.

13 SOCIAL STRATIFICATION

DEFINING SOCIAL STRATIFICATION

All sociologists agree that societies are stratified, or arranged along many levels. Where they begin to differ is on the question of what, if anything, the layers represent beyond the distinctions made among differing degrees of power, wealth, and social prestige.

Stratification and inequality are consistent with an orientation toward society; it is claimed that all societies make distinctions between people. There are some distinctions that always receive differential treatment—as between old and young, or male and female. There are other distinctions that may or may not receive differential treatment depending upon a given society's values. The usual result of a society treating people differently on the basis of their age, sex, race, religion, sexual orientation, or education is social inequality. This inequality can take the form of an unfair distribution of wealth, prestige, or power.

Social stratification represents the structured inequality characterized by groups of people with differential access to the rewards of society because of their relative position in the social hierarchy. Thus, a fundamental task of sociology is the determination of why stratified societies are so prevalent. With almost the entire human population living in such societies, sociologists must try to decide whether stratification is inevitable, and if so, what the effects of social inequality might be.

LIFE CHANCES

Sociologists have found that those in the same social stratum generally share the same life chances or opportunities. They seem to benefit or suffer equally from whatever advantages or disadvantages society has to offer.

STRATIFICATION AND SOCIAL STRUCTURE

Consistent with an orientation toward social structure, stratification systems serve to rank some people (whether individuals or groups) as more deserving of power, wealth, and prestige than others.

Social Hierarchy

The inevitable result of this stratification is a **social hierarchy** of ranked statuses in which people function. These statuses may be either ascribed or achieved. An ascribed social position is either received at birth, or involuntarily placed upon an individual later in life. An acheived social position is usually assumed voluntarily, and generally reflects personal ability or effort. Individuals in a society are treated differently depending on where their social position stands in the overall social hierarchy.

Social Mobility

Social mobility refers to the ability of a given individual or group to move through the social strata. Structural mobility refers to factors at the societal level that affect mobility rates. For example, the number and types of available jobs, dependent on changes in the economic system, have a profound effect on social mobility. In addition, the number of people available to fill those jobs will fluctuate depending on current birthrates and the changing birthrates of previous generations.

Social mobility may be either relative or absolute. An example of relative mobility would be an entire occupational structure being upgraded such that only the content of the work changes, not relative position in the social hierarchy from one generation to the next. An example of absolute mobility would be when a son's education, occupational prestige, and income exceeds that of his father.

SYSTEMS OF STRATIFICATION

A system of stratification refers to the institutions and ideas that permit or limit the distribution of prestige, status, and opportunities in life. Based on the degree of significance attached to certain values in a particular society at a particular time, and the extent to which a particular group monopolizes the areas in which the values are available as evidenced by the development or decline of institutions, stratification may have several sources. These sources include race, ethnicity, gender, age, and sexual orientation—which at times have served as the basis for assigning inferior or superior status to an entire population.

Race and Ethnicity

As sociologists use the term, **race** is more than a biologically complex phenomenon in that it involves the attribution of hereditary differences to human populations that are genetically distinct. The more than 5 billion people living in the world today display an array of physical characteristics—hair color, skin color, eye color and shape, height, weight, facial features, etc. That we categorize people into "races" is a social phenomenon rather than a biological one. In fact, the biological term for race is meaningless. Society, not biology, categorizes people into "races."

Ethnicity refers to a population known and identified on the basis of their common language, national heritage, and/or biological inheritance. Although race primarily refers to differences in physical characteristics, ethnic differences are culturally learned and not genetically inherited.

Gender

Gender stratification refers to those differences between men and women that have been acquired or learned and, hence, to the different roles and positions assigned to males and females in a society. Gender encompasses differences in hairstyle, in the types and styles of clothing worn, and in family and occupational roles. Across societies women have been systematically denied certain rights and opportunities based on assumptions regarding their abilities. This inferior status of women has often been legitimized through a sexist ideology (a belief system assuming that innate characteristics translate into one gender being superior to another) which is passed on across generations via culture.

Age

Age stratification refers to the ways in which people are differentially treated depending on their age. This form of stratification is concerned with the attitudes and behavior we associate with age, and to the different roles and statuses we assign to people depending upon their age.

Sexual Orientation

Stratification on the basis of sexual orientation or affection refers to the ways in which individuals are differentially treated on the basis of their sexual preferences. In some societies, the results of this stratification are relatively benign. However, results of this stratification have also taken the form of criminalization of same sex unions, as well as discrimination in housing, employment, and social status. Many societies forbid homosexual marriages, thereby systematically excluding homosexual couples from the social and economic benefits of marriage. In addition, this exclusion from major social institutions has often translated into a perceived social condonation of discrimination against homosexuals.

DAVIS AND MOORE—A FUNCTIONALIST VIEW OF SOCIAL-STRATIFICATION

In their classic presentation of the functionalist view of stratification, Kingsley Davis and Wilbert Moore (1945) argue that some stratification is necessary. Not everyone has the same abilities. At any given time, some members of a society will have more of the qualities that are needed and desired than others. Also some roles will be more essential to the society's functioning effectively than others. Thus, in order to attract the appropriate people with the requisite talents and skills to the more demanding, often stressful, roles that are not only essential to a society's functioning effectively but that also involve prolonged training and sacrifice, a society must offer greater rewards and higher status. In this way inequality (the unequal distribution of social rewards) is considered functional for society in that it guarantees that those most able will be in the most demanding positions. Social stratification, in other words, is inevitable.

MARX, WEBER, AND MODERN CONFLICT THEORY

Marx attributed inequalities of wealth, power, and prestige to the economic situation that class structures present. Thus, the elimination of classes would serve to put an end to inequality, to the exploitation of man by man, and to the basic conflict of interest between the haves and the have nots. According to Marx, the elimination of class structure would also enable men and women to regain their humanity through the creation of a genuine or true community "where individuals gain their freedom in and through their association."

By contrast, Weber distinguished between class, status situation, and parties as a step toward explaining the origins of the different economic, social, political, and religious situations of society that he saw in India, China, ancient Greece, and Rome, and in the West extending from Great Britain to Russia. By class he meant economic situation as defined by wealth, property, and other opportunities for income. A status situation consisted of every aspect of a person's situation in life that is caused by a positive or negative social assessment of status. Parties were groups oriented toward acquiring social power, i.e., opportunities to realize their common goals despite resistance.

Focused on the origins of man-made culture, Weber often found such differences to be a source of conflict and change that he could not foresee ending. He discovered various systems of stratification. Some were modes of organization based on caste, where social mobility is not permitted by religious sanctions. Others were based on class, including the feudal system of medieval society that was based on vassalage, or reciprocal obligations of loyalty and service between lord and knight or lord and serfs.

Modern conflict theory continues to struggle with the question of the bases of conflict. Believing that Marx placed too much emphasis on class, Ralf Dahrendorf (1959) focused on the struggle among such groups as unions and employers. Randall Collins continues to focus on the way that different groups seek to maintain their social position by acquiring educational credentials that they then use to secure jobs and other advantages. And still others see the conflict over ideological hegemony, including beliefs, attitudes, and ideals, as being the decisive element distinguishing the higher from the lower strata.

14 COLLECTIVE BEHAVIOR

DEFINING COLLECTIVE BEHAVIOR

Collective behavior means group behavior which, though rarely random, generally occurs in the absence of clearly defined and conventional norms. Such behavior may arise spontaneously and is less stable than institutionalized forms of collective behavior. As such, collective behavior generally lacks institutional backing and represents a collective response to changed cultural or social circumstances. Sporadic and short-lived or relatively continuous and longer lasting, collective behavior can be hard to predict because it does not arise in response to cultural or social norms. For this reason, it is even more difficult to observe or measure objectively because it is always in a continual state of flux.

SPONTANEOUS EXPRESSIONS OF COLLECTIVE BEHAVIOR

Collective behavior, which is relatively spontaneous, includes both short-lived spontaneous public expressions of feeling without clear cut goals, and longer lasting public expressions that are aimed at being instrumental in achieving clear-cut goals. Such behavior includes mass hysteria, panics, crazes, fads, fashions, and rumors.

Mass Hysteria

Mass hysteria represents a collective emotional response to tension and anxiety in a group. Such a response cannot be controlled and involves deep-seated emotions on the part of group members who, feeling deprived or powerless, may be responding to such feelings.

Panic

A **panic**, in the sense that sociologists use the term, is a collective action caused by the overwhelming feeling and awareness of needing to escape a dangerous situation immediately. For example, when a fire breaks out in a movie theater, few social norms exist that specify an appropriate action to take. The result may be people panicking and trampling one another in an attempt to escape.

Craze

A **craze** is a situation of collective behavior in which people become obsessed with wanting something because of the popular belief that "everyone else" seems to have it.

Fad

A **fad** represents the type of short-term obsession with a behavior that is unexpected and widely copied, like streaking.

Fashion

Unlike the obsessions with mannerisms, clothes, objects, and speech that crazes and fads represent, **fashions** are more widely held beliefs, styles, and attitudes toward dress, hair styles, music, etc. They usually spread throughout the general population and last longer.

Rumor

A **rumor** is a piece of unconfirmed public information that may or may not be accurate. Typically the source of the rumor is anonymous.

OTHER FORMS OF COLLECTIVE BEHAVIOR— CROWDS

Crowd means a relatively large number of people in close proximity to one another, reacting at once to a common interest or focus. Some examples of crowds include spectators at a football game, participants at a parade, and rioters. There is milling on the part of crowd participants whose physical movements not only express restlessness and excitement, but also are the basis for communication that results in the situation becoming collectively defined and action becoming collectively initiated. As members of an anonymous crowd, people tend to be open to suggestion and to feel a sense of urgency. However, crowds are not completely void of structure. Even when rioting, participants conform to specific patterns of behavior.

Masses

A **mass** refers to those people who are similarly concerned with the same problem or phenomena without necessarily being together in the same place at the same time.

Audiences and Mobs

An **audience** is the type of "passive crowd" that is both oriented toward and responding to a social situation (concert, lecture, sporting event, religious service, burning building) in a relatively orderly and predictable way. A **mob** is the type of crowd that is easily aroused and easily bent to taking aggressive action of a violent or disruptive nature. A **riot**, generally speaking, is not as spontaneous as a mob action, even though riots tend to involve larger numbers of people and usually last longer.

OTHER ASPECTS OF COLLECTIVE BEHAVIOR— PUBLIC VERSUS PRIVATE

The public represents those people in a population with a general interest in and opinion about an issue of concern to them. Public opinion refers to the actual opinions people have about a given issue. Propaganda refers to those attempts to affect and change what the public sees and how the public perceives an issue.

EXPLAINING COLLECTIVE BEHAVIOR

Social scientists have attempted to make sense of unconventional collective behavior over the last century. Contagion, convergence, and emergent-norm theories have been most successful in achieving that end.

Contagion Theory

Contagion theory, developed by Gustave LeBon, contends that crowds exert a distinct milieu that powerfully influences its members. A crowd, made up of numerous anonymous individuals, frees its members of personal responsibility and social restraints. The individual members then succumb to the collective mind of the crowd.

Convergence Theory

Convergence theory posits that the individuals, not the crowd, possess particular motivations. When a number of like-minded individuals converge, they are likely to generate a collective action. For example, rioters in Los Angeles may have all been reacting to feelings of oppression and racism, as embodied by the acquittal of police officers accused of beating black motorist Rodney King. The rioters emerged from a convergence of people sharing a desire for racial equality.

Emergent-Norm Theory

Emergent-norm theory, developed by Ralph Turner and Lewis Killian (1987), argues that crowds do not necessarily begin with individuals sharing the same interests and motives. Instead, certain individuals construct new norms, which are soon adopted by the entire collective. An example is when an individual throws a rock at a policeman and a number of others follow suit. Others may follow shortly after because a new set of expected behaviors (norms) has been created.

SOCIAL MOVEMENTS

A social movement is constituted by a set of beliefs, opinions, interests, and practices generally favoring institutional change of a particular or more general sort. In this context, a countermovement exists when members of a population have opinions and beliefs that they act on in a way which shows their opposition to a particular movement. Institutionalization is the process whereby the ideas of those involved in a social movement come to be known and accepted, serving as the foundation of social organization. Goal displacement occurs when the original goals of a movement are rejected or set aside in favor of the goal of preserving formal structures.

Social movement organizations are those formal organizations that are specifically created for the purpose of channeling either dissatisfaction and discontent into change, or satisfaction and contentment into conservation of tradition. This occurs both at the public level of government policy and at the private level of real concrete action.

PRACTICE
TEST 1

CLEP INTRODUCTORY SOCIOLOGY
Test 1

(Answer sheets appear in the back of this book.)

TIME: 90 Minutes
         100 Questions

> **DIRECTIONS**: Each of the questions or incomplete statements below is followed by five possible answers or completions. Select the best choice in each case and fill in the corresponding oval on the answer sheet.

1. Which of the following is the best example of ethnocentrism?

   (A) We travel to another country and realize their practice of worshipping many gods is both primitive and ignorant.

   (B) We travel to a new society and find it difficult to adjust to the new food and language.

   (C) We find the practice of eating raw fish by the Japanese as unappealing.

   (D) People move to a new state expecting to find more job opportunities. When they arrive and discover it does not work out that way, they become frustrated.

   (E) John meets a student from Brazil and finds the student's culture fascinating.

2. Sally, who comes from a poor black family, finished college and graduate school to become a nuclear physicist. For Sally, being a nuclear physicist is a(n)

   (A) master status.

   (B) achieved status.

   (C) status attainment.

   (D) ascribed status.

   (E) status hierarchy.

3. Stephanie, a plastic surgeon, finds time in her busy schedule to play on a soccer team and attend weekly church functions. Her church and soccer activities make up her

    (A) subordinate statuses.

    (B) master statuses.

    (C) role inconsistencies.

    (D) ascribed statuses.

    (E) None of the above.

4. Concerning the density of social networks, studies suggest that

    I.   dense social networks are positively related to mental and physical health.

    II. dense social networks are positively related to self-esteem.

    III. loose social networks are causally related to poor health.

    IV. gender is causally related to dense social networks.

    (A) I only.

    (B) III only.

    (C) IV only.

    (D) I and II only.

    (E) I, II, and III only.

5. The most radical and complete resocialization is achieved in

    (A) a total institution.

    (B) a bureaucracy.

    (C) late adolescence.

    (D) a subculture.

    (E) None of the above.

6. Which of the following is the best example of Durkheim's theory of anomic suicide?

    (A) After divorcing his wife and moving away from his family, feeling lonely and depressed, Tom decides to kill himself.

    (B) The massive political and economic changes accompanying the breakup of the Soviet Union has resulted in an increased number of suicides among Russian citizens.

    (C) Bob, a captured terrorist, chooses to commit suicide rather than reveal the secrets of his organization.

    (D) Feeling isolated and lonely her first year away at college, Jane decides to kill herself.

    (E) Susan, a member of the Branch Davidian cult, commits mass suicide with the other members of her organization.

7. The _____ perspective would probably try to understand a problem like drug abuse by looking to the power relations between those who abuse drugs and those who do not.

   * (A) conflict

   (B) functionalist

   (C) sociological

   (D) capitalist

   (E) socialist

8. In order to find out more about seatbelt-wearing behavior, John stands unnoticed on a corner and marks down the sex and car type of those who do and do not wear seat belts. He is conducting

   (A) a survey.

   (B) obtrusive research.

   * (C) unobtrusive research.

   (D) experimental research.

   (E) participant-observation research.

9. Social stratification is a profoundly important subject because

   I. almost every aspect of our lives, from family size to occupational aspirations to eating habits, is linked to our position in the social hierarchy.

   II. most societies are committed to the elimination of structured inequality.

   III. a significant reduction in our life chances will occur if we are members of the social hierarchy.

   IV. people in pre-industrial societies are less status-conscious than people in post-industrial societies.

   (A) I only.

   (B) II only.

   (C) I and III only.

   * (D) II and IV only.

   (E) I, II, and IV only.

10. In some groups where the practice of infanticide has resulted in a shortage of eligible female marriage partners, the practice of _____ is relatively common.

(A) polyandry   (D) polygyny

* (B) polygamy   (E) monogamy

(C) exogamy

11. According to Paula, the norms and values of her culture are more rational and advanced than the norms and values of other cultures she has come into contact with. Paula is

(A) stereotyping another culture.

(B) expressing prejudice.

• (C) being ethnocentric.

(D) expressing individual discrimination.

(E) selectively perceiving those events which reinforce her stereotype.

12. A lawyer whose client is convicted of selling marijuana argues against sending the first time offender to prison because of the likelihood of his learning more about crime. Which theory of deviance best supports his argument?

(A) Strain theory

(B) Labeling theory

(C) Control theory

• (D) Cultural transmission theory

(E) Deviance theory

13. The Sapir-Whorf hypothesis suggests that speakers of different languages

• (A) are predisposed to holding contrasting ideals and behaviors due to their divergent linguistic backgrounds.

(B) can perceive the world in identical ways.

(C) hold the same ideas and values due to the cognitive process of learning language.

(D) are predisposed to certain attitudes and interpretations of reality through language.

(E) None of the above.

14. Research on children in isolation suggests that

    (A) with little or no interaction, children can develop fairly normally.

    (B) socialization plays a role in human development.

    • (C) continual human interaction is necessary for normal human development.

    (D) genetics is almost wholly responsible for human development.

    (E) None of the above.

15. According to Goffman, a professor presenting herself to her students as competent and knowledgeable is involved in

    (A) status inconsistency.

    • (B) impression management activities.

    (C) skilled cooperation.

    (D) status performance.

    (E) None of the above.

16. According to sociologists, an important difference between folkways and mores is that

    (A) violation of a folkway leads to severe punishment.

    (B) mores are found only among the upper classes.

    • (C) folkways include customary behaviors.

    (D) violations of mores are not considered crimes.

    (E) folkways apply only to sexual behavior.

17. During pre-modern times when agricultural societies prevailed, in order to increase the supply of labor, couples often had many children. Because today large families are an economic burden rather than an economic asset, couples have fewer children. This explanation of family size is most consistent with the _____ theory in sociology.

    (A) conflict   (D) micro

    • (B) functional   (E) institutional

    (C) symbolic interaction

18. Studies show that as one's education level increases, prejudice decreases, illustrating a _____ relationship between education and prejudice.

    (A) spurious

    • (B) definitive

    (C) causal

    (D) positive correlation

    (E) negative correlation

19. A researcher studying the diaries of Holocaust victims would be using which method to carry out her research?

    (A) A survey

    (B) Participant observation

    (C) Obtrusive research

    • (D) Content analysis

    (E) None of the above.

20. Newpark is a diverse town, both ethnically and racially. The distribution of wealth and earnings among the town members tends to be similar, regardless of race or ethnicity. In Newpark prejudice is

    (A) likely to develop due to the competitive atmosphere.

    (B) likely to develop due to the presence of many racial and ethnic groups.

    (C) less likely to develop due to the inequality existing among groups.

    • (D) less likely to develop due to the economic parity and equality among the groups.

    (E) None of the above.

21. After centuries of occupying a subordinate status and being exploited by the "Plorn," the "Zorn" attempt to form their own country, separate from the "Plorn." Their movement can be classified as

    (A) pluralist.

    (B) assimilationist.

    • (C) segregationist.

    (D) expulsion.

    (E) None of the above.

22. An informal sanction of shoplifting would be

    • (A) receiving a fine from the store.

    (B) a judge requiring you to perform 20 hours of community service.

(C) your date Friday night canceling because he doesn't want to be seen with a thief.

(D) imprisonment for a week.

(E) All of the above.

23. Dr. Shaw is an expert on African religions. She finds the widespread religious practice of performing clitoridectomies on young girls to be disturbing, but believes it can be studied and understood, given the social norms and values of the society. Dr. Shaw is adopting an attitude of

(A) cultural relativism.   •(D) ideal ritualism.

(B) multiculturalism.   (E) None of the above.

(C) ethnocentrism.

24. A widespread desire to own toys and dolls based on a particular television show is an example of a

(A) social movement.   •(D) fad.

(B) fashion.   (E) None of the above.

(C) mob.

25. Studies concerning human instincts suggest that

•(A) many aspects of culture are transmitted genetically in the form of instincts.

(B) human beings do not inherit complex patterns of social behavior and, therefore, have no true instincts.

(C) among people of primitive societies, instincts can be observed.

(D) humans are instinctively aggressive.

(E) sexual behavior is the only genetically transmitted instinct.

26. Researchers decide to test the correlation between the effects of a film on race relations with students' level of prejudice. In this case, the level of prejudice is the _____ variable.

(A) dependent   •(D) spurious

(B) independent   (E) None of the above.

(C) control

27. In order to learn about a particular social phenomenon, Max Weber believed one needed to understand the point of view of the subject. The term used to describe this method is

    (A) social view.
    (D) *verstehen.*
    (B) the looking-glass self.
    (E) social statics.
    (C) symbolic interaction.

28. Which of the following perspectives would focus on how the prosecution and defense interpret each other's actions in a criminal trial?

    (A) Structural functionalism
    (D) Socialization
    (B) Social conflict
    (E) Symbolic interactionism
    (C) Ethnocentrism

29. Which of the following are forms of institutional discrimination?

    I.   A geographic mismatch between workers and jobs following the move of a company from the inner-city.

    II.   A landlord's distaste for Latino tenants causes him to reject all applicants with Hispanic surnames.

    III. During an economic downturn, a policy of "last hired = first fired" has resulted in a disproportionate layoff of women and minorities.

    IV.   The administration of IQ and other standardized tests.

    (A) I only.
    (D) I, III, and IV only.
    (B) I and II only.
    (E) I, II, III, and IV.
    (C) II and III only.

30. Which of the following is true of welfare recipients?

    (A) The majority are women who have many children.
    (B) Most are males who are unwilling to work.
    (C) Most are children.
    (D) Few ever get off welfare.
    (E) None of the above.

31. Regarding segregation, studies indicate that

   I.   blacks show a preference for segregation and prefer to live in predominantly black neighborhoods.

   II. whites prefer to maintain a segregated system in terms of public accommodations and housing.

   III. blacks, more than whites, prefer to live in integrated neighborhoods.

   IV. whites, more than blacks, prefer to live in integrated neighborhoods.

   (A) I only.   (D) I and II only.

   (B) II only.   (E) None of the above.

   (C) III only.

32. Which of the following is best explained by the Strain theory?

   (A) Voyeurism   (D) Speeding

   (B) Marijuana use   (E) Jaywalking

   (C) Robbery

33. One reason lower class youth are more often arrested than individuals of other social classes is that

   (A) they commit more dangerous crimes.

   (B) there are greater numbers of police in their neighborhoods.

   (C) police are guided by particular status cues such as demeanor, dress, and race.

   (D) they are more likely to commit crimes that are reported.

   (E) they commit more of all types of crimes.

34. A professor has certain rights and obligations associated with her status, such as meeting with her students and preparing lectures. These rights and obligations associated with a status are known as

   (A) master statuses.   (D) roles.

   (B) ascribed statuses.   (E) impression management.

   (C) achieved statuses.

35. Cindy and Bobby, two siblings playing house, pretend they are their parents. According to George Herbert Mead, Cindy and Bobby are learning to internalize the values of their parents and are therefore taking on the role of the

    (A) instinctual being.   (D) *verstehen.*

    •(B) socialized other.   (E) generalized other.

    (C) looking-glass self.

36. A general difficulty confronted in doing social research is that

    I.   ethical considerations prevent certain types of research from taking place.

    II.   it deals with subjects who are self-aware and whose behavior is not always predictable.

    III. social researchers are part of the phenomenon they study.

    IV.   the methods of social research are more advanced than those of other disciplines.

    (A) II only.   (D) I and III only.

    (B) III only.   •(E) I, II, and III only.

    (C) IV only.

37. In order to get a sample of Los Angeles residents for a survey on political attitudes, Carmen selects every 1000th person from the Los Angeles city phone book. This is an example of _____ sampling.

    (A) random   (D) stratified

    •(B) systematic   (E) non-representative

    (C) cluster

38. Sally, a social researcher studying education level and condom use, finds subjects who graduate from college are no more likely to use condoms than those who do not graduate from college. Her findings suggest that

    (A) education and condom use are positively correlated.

    (B) education and condom use are negatively correlated.

(C) a cause-and-effect relationship exists between education level and condom use.

• (D) no apparent relationship exists between the two variables.

(E) a spurious relationship exists between the two variables.

39. The sociologist's interest in race is due to the fact that

I.   race, as a biological fact, helps to determine and explain people's behavior.

II. stratification on the basis of race predates all other forms of stratification.

III. people attach meaning and values to real or imagined group differences.

IV. race is the basis for discrimination against all minority groups.

(A) I only.   (D) II and IV only.

• (B) III only.   (E) None of the above.

(C) I and II only.

40. The "Zorn," an ethnic group in the country of "Plorn," migrated voluntarily more than three centuries ago. Over time, they have completely adopted the norms, values, and language of the dominant group. Contact between the two groups, however, is still somewhat limited. "Zorns" have only some political representation, and economic inequality, though not drastic, still exists. Intermarriage between the two groups is remarkably low, and neighborhoods are not well integrated. "Zorn" assimilation can be characterized as

(A) low cultural assimilation; low structural assimilation.

(B) moderate cultural assimilation; moderate secondary structural assimilation; low primary structural assimilation.

(C) moderate cultural assimilation; low structural assimilation.

(D) high cultural assimilation; moderate secondary structural assimilation; low primary structural assimilation.

(E) high cultural assimilation; moderate secondary structural assimilation; moderate primary structural assimilation.

41. The gap between male and female earnings is due to which of the following?

    I.   The failure of bosses to perceive women as competent and capable.

    • II.   Differences in how jobs are titled/labeled when filled by one sex rather than the other.

    • III.   The preference of all men to have their wives work in the home rather than in the labor market.

    IV.   Women generally have less experience and skills, causing them to enter low-paying, female-dominated occupations.

(A) I only.

(B) I and III only.

(C) III and IV only.

(D) II, III, and IV only.

• (E) I, II, and IV only.

42. As Tom's perpetual tardiness becomes disturbing to the class, the other students scorn him. The behavior of the students is an example of a(n)

• (A) informal sanction.

(B) formal sanction.

(C) norm.

(D) value.

(E) None of the above.

43. Recent studies suggest power over and subordination of another are most likely to be the motivations for which of the following crimes?

    • I.   Car theft

    . II.   Embezzlement

    III.   Rape

    IV.   Jaywalking

(A) I only.

(B) III only.

(C) I and II only.

• (D) I, II, and III only.

(E) I, II, III, and IV.

44. The type of social cohesion that binds people who do similar work and have a similar world view is referred to by Durkheim as

(A) organic solidarity. • (D) virtual solidarity.

(B) mechanical solidarity. (E) None of the above.

(C) cohesive solidarity.

45. A sociologist is interested in studying American college students' opinions on euthanasia. What is the population of her study?

(A) College students on her campus

(B) The students randomly chosen for a response

(C) All college students

(D) An individual student

(E) All people between the ages of 18-21

46. Research shows an inverse relationship between levels of education and extent of prejudice. As far as we know today, which of the following most likely accounts for at least some of that relationship?

   I.   People who are less educated have greater contact with people of various ethnic and racial groups, thereby making them less prejudiced.

   II. As people attain more education they become more tolerant.

   III. People who are prejudice are less likely to pursue a higher education.

 • IV. As people become more educated, they are more careful about revealing their prejudices.

(A) I only.   (D) I and II only.

(B) II only.   (E) II and IV only.

(C) IV only.

47. Rigid endogamy is associated with which type of system?

(A) Stratification   •(D) Polygamous

(B) Class   (E) None of the above.

(C) Caste

48. Opponents of affirmative action argue which of the following?

 • I. Enhancing the opportunities for one group means unfairly limiting the opportunities of another.

 II. Such programs only help those minorities who are skilled and educated, and do little to help those who are poor and lack skills.

 • III. Race consciousness and conflict will be more acute as job opportunities for non-minorities are lessened.

 (A) I only.   • (D) I and III only.

 (B) II only.   (E) I, II, and III.

 (C) III only.

49. In Boston, an Irish-American community exists, complete with a distinctive religion and ethnic lifestyle. This group can be categorized as a(n)

 (A) counterculture.   (D) ethnocentric culture.

 (B) non-material culture.   (E) deviant subculture.

 • (C) subculture.

50. Which of the following would be considered a defining characteristic of a closed stratification system?

 (A) There are rigid boundaries between classes that are difficult or impossible for people to cross.

 (B) Immigration from other nations is not allowed.

 (C) The boundaries between classes are poorly defined, and people can cross them unnoticed.

 (D) Hereditary position plays little role in determining a person's position in the stratification system.

 • (E) Achieved status is more important than ascribed status in determining a person's position in the stratification system.

51. Which of the following lists of characteristics best illustrates ascribed statuses?

    (A) Female, Asian, Olympic athlete

    (B) Male, Jewish, rabbi

    (C) Female, married, pregnant

    (D) Female, age 27, pediatrician

    (E) Male, African-American, age 45

52. Early sociological arguments addressing the different social positions of ethnic groups were generally rooted in Darwinism, meaning that

    (A) groups were ranked hierarchically on the basis of skin color, with lighter skinned ethnic groups occupying positions superior to darker skinned groups.

    (B) different positions were explained as reflecting a difference in genetics.

    (C) cultural values dictated where an ethnic group was located, with those groups possessing values of hard work and education occupying higher positions than those lacking such values.

    (D) factors such as "selective migration" best explained an ethnic group's level of success upon arrival.

    (E) None of the above.

53. Marx referred to the owners of the means of production as the

    (A) owners.   (D) proletariat.

    (B) bourgeoisie.   (E) upper class.

    (C) elite.

54. Which of the following ethnic groups has an unemployment rate often exceeding 50 percent?

    (A) African-Americans   (D) American Indians

    (B) Asian-Americans   •(E) All of the above.

    (C) Latinos

55. One of the dysfunctions of the nuclear family is that

    •(A) children are viewed as an economic liability as opposed to an economic benefit.

    (B) married couples may be deprived of support from other relatives.

    (C) family size hinders group mobility.

    (D) gender roles are less rigid than in other family forms.

    (E) All of the above.

56. Evidence regarding teacher-student interactions and student performance suggests

    (A) teachers have little influence on students' self-concepts.

    • (B) teacher expectation greatly influences student performance.

    (C) teachers have little or no influence on student performance.

    (D) teachers influence all students equally.

    (E) the student alone determines academic performance.

57. John, who is 15, will be entering the labor market shortly after the turn of the century. In which sector will he be most likely to get a job?

    (A) Manufacturing   (D) International

    (B) Agricultural   •(E) Government

    (C) Service

58. Religion, according to Karl Marx, is

    I.   an institution of the elite.

    II. the center of all conflict.

III. appealing to the masses because it provides an escape from reality.

(A) I only.

(D) II and III only.

(B) II only.

•(E) I, II, and III.

•(C) III only.

59. Which of the following contributed to the early growth of suburbs?

(A) Decrease in birth rate

(B) Decline in agriculture

(C) Increased population of rural areas

— (D) Advances in transportation

•(E) All of the above.

60. In developing nations, the problem of _____ often occurs in cities where the population grows faster than the supply of housing and jobs.

(A) industrialization

(D) over-urbanization

•(B) gentrification

(E) None of the above.

(C) under-urbanization

61. Regarding the census, information on _____ is often not included.

(A) elderly

•(D) students

— (B) illegal aliens

(E) All of the above.

(C) prisoners

62. John grows up in a society founded upon prejudicial and racist principles. He internalizes these prejudicial values and norms, eventually becoming prejudiced himself. What theory best explains why John is prejudiced?

•(A) Power-conflict

(B) Frustration-aggression

(C) Authoritarian personality

(D) Scapegoat

(E) Normative

63. Immigration policy throughout the early part of this century maintained a quota system, meaning that

• (A) those groups possessing greater skills and education were favored.

(B) those groups in a position to easily assimilate were favored.

(C) those groups coming from predominantly Catholic countries were prohibited from entering.

(D) Chinese immigrants were prohibited from entering.

(E) None of the above.

64. Sue, a tenured professor at an elite college, accepts an offer to teach at another elite college. Her move is an example of

(A) horizontal mobility.

(B) vertical mobility.

(C) intergenerational mobility.

• (D) status mobility.

(E) None of the above.

65. Which of the following are forms of institutional discrimination addressed by affirmative action?

• I. Rules requiring that only English be spoken in the workplace.

• II. Restrictive employment leave policies which work against employed mothers.

• III. Credit policies which prevent lending in minority neighborhoods.

IV. Landlords who overtly refuse to rent to minorities.

(A) I only.

(B) II only.

(C) I and IV only.

• (D) I, II, and III.

(E) I, II, III, and IV.

66. Which of the following is the most accurate statement about secularization and the future of religion in the United States today?

    • (A) We are becoming increasingly more secularized, and the role of religion is diminishing.

    (B) The role of the other institutions, such as government, science, and education, have completely taken over the role of religion.

    (C) In spite of the changes occurring, the institution of religion remains a fundamental component of every society.

    (D) Religion is an important institution mainly among the working class.

    (E) None of the above.

67. Larry's math placement test shows he should be in the high math group. Larry's teachers are using a

    (A) stratification system.   (D) bureaucratic system.

    (B) tracking system.   (E) None of the above.

    (C) tiered system.

68. The primary reason corporations establish subsidiaries in other countries is to

    (A) acquire cheaper natural resources.

    (B) acquire more land.

    (C) assist in development.

    (D) acquire cheaper labor and taxes.

    • (E) All of the above.

69. Mr. Clark, a kindergarten teacher, has his students say the pledge of allegiance and sing "America the Beautiful" everyday before class. He is teaching his students about American

    (A) religion.   • (D) civil religion.

    (B) secularization.   (E) None of the above.

    (C) socialism.

70. Bob wants to move to the suburbs but is unable to do so. Bob is probably

    (A) poor and less educated.

    (B) educated and elderly.

    (C) middle class and less educated.

    (D) white and middle class.

    (E) working class and elderly.

71. Newpark, an old rundown part of the city, has recently been bought by a wealthy businessman who has repaired the area and is now renting to mainly white, middle-class professionals. This process is referred to as

    (A) industrialization.   (D) suburbanization.

    (B) over-urbanization.   (E) centralization.

    (C) gentrification.

72. Stratification on the basis of race

    I.   is based on biological differences in groups of people which are translated, genetically, into different behavioral and personality traits.

    II. is synonymous with slavery since historically people have been enslaved on the basis of skin color.

    III. has often been justified by an ideology (racism) which contends that some races are innately superior to others.

    IV. is insignificant compared to other stratification systems such as those based on age or gender.

    (A) I only.   (D) I and IV only.

    (B) II only.   (E) I, II, III, and IV.

    (C) III only.

73. The "culture of poverty" concept attempts to explain poverty in all of the following ways except

    (A) the values of the poor are responsible for their poverty.

(B) poverty is passed from one generation to the next due to flaws inherent to their culture.

(C) laziness and a present-time orientation create poverty.

(D) structural barriers prevent some people from attaining an adequate economic position.

(E) All of the above.

74. Regarding prejudice, the authoritarian-personality theory of aggression is best at explaining

(A) extreme prejudicial attitudes of a few.

(B) how prejudicial attitudes are transmitted across generations.

(C) the benefits a dominant group receives by subjugating a minority group.

(D) why all people, to some degree, have prejudices.

(E) None of the above.

75. In most pre-industrial societies, marriage is viewed as

I. a formal arrangement between individuals who are bonded by romantic love.

II. a polygamous arrangement between three individuals.

III. a formal arrangement between two individuals who share similar social characteristics.

IV. a practical economic arrangement.

(A) I only.   (D) II, III, and IV only.

(B) IV only.   (E) None of the above.

(C) II and IV only.

76. Which of the following is true of family violence?

I. Husbands who abuse their wives are largely concentrated in the working class.

II. Women are more likely than men to suffer serious injuries as a result of family violence.

III. Almost one-third of women who are murdered are killed by spouses, ex-spouses, or unmarried partners.

IV. Men who abuse their wives and/or children are often abused themselves.

(A) I only.

(D) II, III, and IV only.

(B) IV only.

(E) I, II, III, and IV.

(C) II and IV only.

77. Workers with a high degree of autonomy report

(A) lower salaries.

(D) greater job satisfaction.

(B) being unchallenged.

(E) None of the above.

(C) less job satisfaction.

78. Which of the following characteristics best describes the group least likely to vote?

(A) White; under 40; receptionist earning $17,000/year

(B) Asian; over 40; bar owner earning $42,000/year

(C) White; under 40; used car salesperson earning $65,000/year

(D) African-American; under 40; professional earning $45,000/year

(E) White; over 40; office manager earning $21,000/year

79. The net increase/decrease of a population depends on which of the following factors?

I. Migration

II. Fertility

III. Mortality

IV. Urbanization

(A) I only.

(D) I and IV only.

(B) II only.

(E) I, II, and III only.

(C) III only.

80. When looking at age-sex population pyramids of the United States and Mexico, one finds that

I. the United States' pyramid is heavy at the bottom and top, but thinner in the middle.

    II.   the Mexican pyramid is heavy at the bottom and top, but thinner in the middle.

    III. men outnumber women in most age groups in both the United States and Mexico.

(A) I only.

(B) II only.

(C) III only.

(D) I and II only.

(E) None of the above.

81. Fecundity can be explained as

(A) the average number of children a woman has over her lifetime.

(B) the number of births per 1,000 women in the population.

(C) the ratio of males to females.

(D) the potential number of children a woman can have during her childbearing years.

(E) None of the above.

82. Efforts to count the homeless have been criticized because

(A) many studies have failed to count the hidden homeless.

(B) most people counted as homeless really are not.

(C) a good portion of those defined as homeless choose to live on the streets.

(D) some studies purposefully undercount the homeless.

(E) All of the above.

83. Which of the following is not a goal of feminism?

(A) To change the present system which provides only limited choices in women's roles

(B) To promote sexual autonomy and the right of women to have great jurisdiction over sexuality and reproduction

(C) To reverse the sexist ideology that claims men are innately superior, and instead, promote the superiority of women

(D) To end violence directed at women

(E) All of the above.

84. When the architectural firm Gary works for merges with another, he leaves his position as office manager and finds a secretarial job in a new office. This is an example of _____ mobility.

    (A) horizontal

    (B) vertical

    (C) intergenerational

    (D) status

    (E) None of the above.

85. Which of the following does the sociology of religion focus on?

    (A) Theological questions, such as the existence of God

    (B) How accurate ideas of the supernatural are

    (C) The ability of the major religions to answer the fundamental questions of our existence

    (D) The social characteristics and consequences of religion

    (E) All of the above.

86. Which of the following characteristics most likely describes Molly, a single mother with two children?

    (A) Molly lives with her grandparents.

    (B) Molly lives with the father of her children.

    (C) Molly lives in an urban area.

    (D) Molly lives at or below the poverty line.

    (E) None of the above.

87. Which of the following lists of characteristics best describes the group with the highest unemployment rate?

    (A) Black; female; over 50

    (B) Black; male; under 50

    (C) White; female; under 50

    (D) Black; male; over 50

    (E) White; male; under 50

88. Regarding voter turnout, the United States can be described as having

    (A) remarkably high voter turnout.

    (B) one of the lowest voter turnouts in the democratic world.

(C) higher voter turnout for people of lower social classes.

(D) low voter turnout among the elderly.

▴ (E) None of the above.

89. The population has boomed in many developing countries because

I. the birth rate has increased dramatically.

II. people from these countries engage in sex more frequently and at younger ages.

III. while the birth rate has remained relatively stable, or declined only slightly, the death rate has dropped sharply.

IV. both birth and death rates have increased sharply.

(A) I only.

(D) I and II only.

▪ (B) III only.

(E) I, II, and IV only.

(C) IV only.

90. Leon, who lives in Alabama, gets a job offer in Colorado where the pay is excellent, living conditions are good, and there are more single women. Leon's decision to migrate is based on

▪ (A) pull factors.

▪(D) demographic factors.

(B) push factors.

(E) None of the above.

(C) industrial factors.

91. Compared to the early suburban population, today's suburbanites are

(A) mostly upper-middle class.

▪ (B) mostly working class.

(C) as diverse as urbanites.

(D) mostly of minority backgrounds.

(E) None of the above.

92. Which of the following have contributed to the increased homeless rate?

I. A shortage of inexpensive housing

II. A decline in public welfare benefits

III. A decline in the demand for unskilled labor

IV. An increase in personal disabilities such as alcoholism

(A) II only.

(B) III only.

(C) II and IV only.

(D) I, II, and III.

(E) I, II, III, and IV.

93. The main cause of the large increase in single-parent families is the

(A) dramatic increase in divorce.

(B) soaring illegitimacy rate.

(C) social pressure to get married once pregnant.

(D) decrease in extended families.

(E) None of the above.

94. Regarding marriage, the majority of couples share which of the following characteristics?

I. Social class background

II. Educational level

III. Racial background

IV. Personality traits

(A) I only.

(B) III only.

(C) III and IV only.

(D) I, II and III only.

(E) I, II, III, and IV.

95. The sacred, according to Emile Durkheim, is the symbolic representation of

(A) Jesus.

(B) the family.

(C) one's parents.

(D) society.

(E) None of the above.

96. Which of the following lists best describes push factors?

(A) Cold climate; good job; close to relatives

(B) Warm climate; loss of a job; close to good schools

(C) Nice neighborhoods; good job; close to good schools

(D) Cold climate; loss of a job; religious persecution

(E) None of the above.

97. Which of the following characteristics best describes people who first moved to suburbs?

(A) Racially and ethnically diverse

(B) Wealthy

(C) Working class

(D) Agricultural workers

(E) None of the above.

98. Because urban and suburban populations have become more alike, an increased number of people have moved

(A) out of the country.

(B) to the snow-belt region.

(C) back to the urban center.

(D) to rural areas.

(E) None of the above.

99. Which of the following equations best illustrates pluralism?

(A) $A + B + C = A$

(B) $A + B + C = D$

(C) $A + B = C + D$

(D) $A + B + C = A + B + C$

(E) None of the above.

100. The extended family declined during industrialization because

(A) living in a small residence, such as an apartment, was preferred to a large residence, such as a house.

(B) greater geographic mobility was required.

(C) economic development meant families were no longer dependent on one another.

(D) the increased wealth accompanying industrialization meant families increased their non-kin relationships.

(E) All of the above.

CLEP INTRODUCTORY SOCIOLOGY
TEST 1

ANSWER KEY

1. (A)	26. (A)	51. (E)	76. (D)
2. (B)	27. (D)	52. (B)	77. (D)
3. (A)	28. (E)	53. (B)	78. (A)
4. (D)	29. (D)	54. (D)	79. (E)
5. (A)	30. (C)	55. (B)	80. (E)
6. (B)	31. (C)	56. (B)	81. (D)
7. (A)	32. (C)	57. (C)	82. (A)
8. (C)	33. (C)	58. (C)	83. (C)
9. (A)	34. (D)	59. (D)	84. (B)
10. (A)	35. (E)	60. (D)	85. (D)
11. (C)	36. (E)	61. (B)	86. (D)
12. (D)	37. (B)	62. (E)	87. (B)
13. (D)	38. (D)	63. (B)	88. (B)
14. (C)	39. (B)	64. (A)	89. (B)
15. (B)	40. (D)	65. (D)	90. (A)
16. (C)	41. (E)	66. (C)	91. (C)
17. (B)	42. (A)	67. (B)	92. (D)
18. (E)	43. (B)	68. (D)	93. (B)
19. (D)	44. (B)	69. (D)	94. (D)
20. (D)	45. (C)	70. (A)	95. (D)
21. (E)	46. (E)	71. (C)	96. (D)
22. (C)	47. (C)	72. (C)	97. (B)
23. (A)	48. (E)	73. (D)	98. (D)
24. (D)	49. (C)	74. (A)	99. (D)
25. (B)	50. (A)	75. (B)	100. (B)

DETAILED EXPLANATIONS OF ANSWERS

TEST 1

1.   **(A)**   Ethnocentric means to judge another culture by the standards of your own and to place yours as superior. Seeing another's practice of worshipping many gods as primitive and ignorant is judging the practice and seeing it as inferior. (B) is not an example of ethnocentrism because having difficulty adjusting to new food and a new language is not judging the practice as inferior. (C) is incorrect. One cannot find a practice unappealing without deeming it inferior. (D) is not an example of ethnocentrism because one does not encounter an entirely new culture when moving across states. (E) is incorrect. Rather than judging Brazilian culture as inferior, John demonstrates an enthusiasm and fascination with this culture.

2.   **(B)**   An achieved status is a social position based largely on one's merit. In this scenario, Sally has become a nuclear physicist, which requires individual merit to achieve. (A) is incorrect. A master status refers to one's central defining characteristic. Although this characteristic is often one's occupation, in our society, race is a more centrally defining characteristic. (C) Status attainment refers to the process by which individuals come to hold a certain position in the stratification system, which is unrelated to this example. (D) is incorrect. An ascribed status refers to a social position based on involuntary characteristics, such as sex, age, and race. In this example, being black and female are Sally's ascribed characteristics. (E) is incorrect, as status hierarchy is not a sociological term.

3.   **(A)**   Subordinate statuses refer to the statuses one occupies that are not the master status. For Stephanie, her status as a soccer player and churchgoer are secondary to her status as a plastic surgeon. (B) is incorrect. Her master status, or her central defining characteristic, is as a plastic surgeon. (C) is incorrect. Role inconsistency refers to the inconsistencies

in the roles associated with a single status. In this example, Stephanie's numerous statuses are being addressed. (D) is incorrect. An ascribed status is an involuntary status, such as sex or race. Stephanie's statuses of churchgoer and soccer player are largely, if not entirely, voluntary statuses. Because a correct answer is provided, (E) is incorrect.

4.   **(D)**   Density of social networks has been shown to be health promoting, both mentally and physically, and a positive influence on self-concept. People reporting numerous close friends have better subjective and objective health ratings. (A) is incorrect as it only contains one of the correct responses. (B) and (E) are incorrect as they both include statement III. Loose social networks are correlated with bad health, but the relationship has not been shown to be causal. We don't know if loose social networks lead to poor health, or if being in poor health leads to fewer social contacts. (C) is incorrect because we cannot ascertain whether the relationship between gender and social networks is causal.

5.   **(A)**   In a total institution, such as a prison or mental hospital, all aspects of an individual's life are controlled, in order to strip down and rebuild the self. (B) is incorrect. A bureaucracy is a large formal organization that does not have as its goal re-socialization and the rebuilding of the self. (C) This process does not occur only in late adolescence, but can occur at any age. People of all ages are resocialized in total institutions. (D) The term subculture refers to a culture within a culture and has no relevance to this example. Because a correct answer is provided, (E) is incorrect.

6.   **(B)**   Durkheim believed that anomic suicide resulted from normlessness. When the norms of a society are suddenly altered, it may result in people's being confused about the boundaries of their society. Only answer (B) addresses the large structural changes occurring in society that may impact the individual. (C) and (E) are examples of altruistic suicide where an individual over identifies with a group and is willing to die for them. (A) and (D) are examples of egoistic suicide, which results from isolation and weak social ties.

7.   **(A)**   The conflict perspective views society as being unequal in terms of power. In this example, the power relations between groups and individuals are being questioned. (B) is incorrect. A functionalist perspective views society's systems as being interrelated and working together to maintain stability. (C), (D), and (E) are not sociological paradigms used to explain social phenomenon.

8. **(C)** In unobtrusive research, no interaction takes place between the researcher and the subject under study. The research in no way attempts to influence the behavior or response of the subject. In this case, John has absolutely no contact with his subjects. (A) A survey is a method used in which subjects respond to a series of questions on a questionnaire. John does not question his subject directly. (B) Obtrusive research is exactly the opposite of what is being done in this example. It is when the researcher has extensive contact with his subject, potentially influencing the response. (D) Experimental research seeks to find cause-effect relationships, and takes place under highly controlled conditions. Nothing in the question indicates an experimental design, so (D) is incorrect. (E) Participant-observation research is when the researcher becomes involved with the subject under study and actually participates in the same behaviors. John does not participate in his subjects' actions.

9. **(A)** Social stratification, or structured inequality, is so vital to understand because every aspect of our lives is influenced by where we fall in the hierarchical system. Our access to socially valued goods and rewards (i.e., money, education) is dependent upon our place in the stratification system. (B) is incorrect. Most societies do not seem committed to the elimination of structured inequality. All societies are stratified, whether by sex, age, or race. (C) is also incorrect. Every individual is born into a system of stratification. Our life chances will be reduced only if we occupy a subordinate position in that hierarchy. (D) and (E) are incorrect because they include statement II, which is wrong.

10. **(A)** Polyandry is the practice of one woman marrying more than one man. In societies where there are fewer women than men, either through warfare or infanticide, the women will be shared by the men. (B) is incorrect. Polygamy refers only to one person marrying two or more other people. The term does not state whether it is the man or woman who has multiple marriages. (C) Exogamy refers to the marriage outside one's group. For example, an African-American who marries an Asian is practicing exogamy. (D) Polygyny refers to one man marrying two or more women. This is opposite from the example. (E) Monogamy refers to a form of marriage where only two partners are involved.

11. **(C)** Ethnocentric means to judge another culture by the standards of one's own. By seeing all other cultures she has come into contact with as inferior, Paula is being ethnocentric. (A) is incorrect. Paula is not stereotyping any one culture, rather she is seeing all other cultures as inferior.

(B) is incorrect. A prejudice is a judgment based on an individual's group membership, not his or her personal attributes. Paula is not judging an individual based on their group membership. Rather, she is making a judgment concerning an entire culture — her own. (D) Paula is not expressing individual discrimination. Discrimination is a behavior, while ethnocentrism is a belief. Paula does not behave unfairly toward another group. She merely holds opinions about many different groups and cultures. (E) Selective perception is selectively perceiving those cases which reinforce your stereotype of a certain group. Paula does not stereotype any single group and does not use any specific examples to reinforce her stereotype.

12. **(D)** Cultural transmission theory contends that crime is learned through cultural and subcultural norms. The lawyer is afraid his client will learn more about crime via the subcultural norms of prison. (A) is incorrect as strain theory does not include a component of learning. Strain theory suggests crime is the result of structural constraints placed on the individual, blocking means for achievement. (B) is incorrect. Labeling theory does not rely on learning to commit crime. Rather, it focuses on the process by which one is labeled and defined as a criminal. (C) is incorrect. Control theory maintains that all of us deviate, and those who do not are more attached to their society. Since no theory termed "deviance theory" exists, (E) is wrong.

13. **(D)** The Sapir-Whorf hypothesis says that people think through language. Language is not just the vehicle through which we express ourselves; language also shapes our thoughts. (A) is incorrect. The Sapir-Whorf hypothesis makes no prediction of behavior of people who speak different languages. (B) states the opposite of the Sapir-Whorf hypothesis because speakers of different languages do not perceive the world in identical ways since perception and ideas vary across languages. (C) According to the Sapir-Whorf hypothesis, speakers of different languages would view the world differently because their language predisposes them to think and perceive in a particular way. Because a correct answer is provided, (E) is incorrect.

14. **(C)** Research on children raised in isolation suggests that in order to develop and be fully human, people need continual interaction. (A) is incorrect as it states nearly the opposite. (B) and (D) are incorrect for the same reason. Both answers suggest that genetics (nature) is more powerful than social processes (nurture). To the contrary, studies show that social

interaction is vital throughout the life course. Because a correct answer is provided, (E) is incorrect.

15. **(B)** Impression management refers to the conscious manipulation of role performance. The professor in this example is manipulating her role performance in order to impress her students. (A) is incorrect. Status inconsistency is a condition in which a person holds a higher position on one dimension of stratification than on another. This example is not addressing different statuses, but the roles associated with a single status. (C) and (D) are both incorrect, as these terms have no sociological meaning. A correct answer is provided, so (E) is incorrect.

16. **(C)** Folkways are social norms governing less important areas of behavior such as table manners or proper attire for events. Mores are social norms which concern more serious issues such as laws against murder or incest. (A) is incorrect since violations of folkways usually result in mild reprimands. (D) is incorrect because violations of mores are usually considered crimes and involve more drastic punishments. (B) and (E) are also incorrect because folkways and mores are found among all social groups and cover a wide range of behaviors.

17. **(B)** A functionalist argument is based on the assumption that society's complex systems work together to maintain stability. In this example, family size is explained as part of a system that is maintaining its stability. (A) is incorrect. A conflict approach assumes conflict and inequality underlie society. This explanation of family size does not discuss the tensions and inequalities that promote social change. (C) The symbolic interactionism approach assumes that society is the product of everyday interactions of people. In this example, individual interaction is never addressed. (D) is incorrect. Rather than being micro, or focusing at the individual level, this explanation is macro, and focuses on the structural level. (E) is incorrect because no sociological term "institutional argument" exists.

18. **(E)** A negative correlation is an association between two variables so that as one increases the other decreases, as is the case with education and prejudice in this example. (A) A spurious relationship is an apparent association that can actually be explained by a third variable. Nothing from this example suggests that a third variable is explaining both prejudice and education levels. (B) is incorrect as no sociological term "definitive" exists. (C) Nothing from this example suggests this relationship is

causal. We cannot say definitively that education level causes prejudice. We only know that a relationship between the two exists. (D) is incorrect. The association would be positive if both variables increased or decreased together.

19. **(D)**   Content analysis is a method in which the researcher uses artifacts and existing data. In this example, the researcher uses a diary to understand more about social behavior. Other examples might be the use of newspapers or song lyrics. (A) A survey is a method in which a subject is asked to respond to a series of questions. (B) and (C) are incorrect. The researcher is not participating or interacting in any way with the subject. Because a correct response is provided, (E) is incorrect.

20. **(D)**   Research on prejudice suggests that in a non-competitive atmosphere, when individuals from different ethnic backgrounds come together, there is likely to be little conflict. In an economically competitive atmosphere, conflict is likely to ensue. (A) is incorrect because in Newpark the distribution of goods is fairly equal. (B) and (C) are incorrect. Diversity leads to conflict when there are dramatic inequalities between groups. In this example, there is economic parity, regardless of race and ethnicity. (E) is incorrect since a correct answer has been provided.

21. **(E)**   By attempting to create their own country, the "Zorn" movement can be classified as secessionist, which is not an answer choice. (A) is incorrect. In a pluralist movement, minority groups attempt to maintain their own distinctive cultural features, while still operating within the larger society. An example would be an Irish-American neighborhood. (B) An assimilationist movement is when the minority completely adopts the culture and way of life of the majority. (C) is incorrect. A segregationist movement is when separate public accommodations (schools, houses, parks, buses, etc.) are set up for minorities, within the same society. Minority groups still function within the larger society and are still subject to the majority's laws and political system. (D) is incorrect. Expulsion is the process whereby the dominant group attempts to force an unwanted population out of their borders. This differs from secession in that in the latter movement, the subordinate group attempts to leave or separate from the dominant group.

22. **(C)**   An informal sanction is direct social pressure from those around us to conform. The term "informal" suggests that the pressure is not coming from a formal or legal institution such as the criminal justice

system. Instead the pressure to conform may be coming from our family or peer group. If your date cancels, the pressure to conform is informal. All of the other choices, (A), (B), and (D) show the role of formal institution in pressuring one to conform, either through fines, imprisonment, or community service. Because (A), (B), and (D) refer to formal sanctions, (E) is incorrect.

23. **(A)** Cultural relativism is the attempt on the part of researchers to not judge another culture by the standards of one's own. By trying to understand the practice of performing clitoridectomies, without judging the practice as bad, or the culture as inferior, Dr. Shaw is adopting an attitude of cultural relativism. (B) Multiculturalism refers to a variety of cultures living in the same society. Dr. Shaw is not studying a culture within her society; therefore, (B) is incorrect. (C) is incorrect. Ethnocentrism refers to the judgment of another culture seeing yours as superior. Dr. Shaw is adopting the opposite approach. (D) is incorrect. No sociological term "ideal ritualism" exists. Because a correct answer has been provided, (E) is incorrect.

24. **(D)** A fad is an unconventional social pattern that people engage in briefly but enthusiastically. (A) is incorrect. A social movement is an organized activity that seeks social change. The interest in such toys and dolls is not organized, and there is no goal of social change. (B) A fashion is a social pattern favored for a long period of time by large numbers of people. The interest is quickly fleeting and therefore does not qualify as a fashion. (C) is incorrect. A mob is a highly emotional crowd that is pursuing a destructive goal. Because a correct answer is provided, (E) is incorrect.

25. **(B)** The variation in behavior cross-culturally suggests that culture and patterns of behavior are not instinctual, or transmitted genetically. Most researchers agree that humans have drives (sex, hunger), but no true instincts, making (A) incorrect. (C) Instincts have never been observed in either primitive societies or developed societies. (D) and (E) are incorrect. While drives do exist, how they are played out varies immensely cross-culturally.

26. **(A)** The dependent variable is the one we are trying to explain. In this question, we are trying to explain the level of prejudice; therefore, it is the dependent variable. (B) is incorrect because the independent variable is the variable doing the explaining (the cause). Since the film is

seen as explaining the level of prejudice, it is the independent variable. (C) is incorrect. The control variable is the variable being held constant so that one can assess the relationship among the other variables. Since level of prejudice is not being held constant in this example, it is not a control variable. A spurious relationship is one where the variables appear to be related, but are actually related to a third variable which explains both of them. Nothing from this example would suggest that the relationship between prejudice and the film is being caused by a third variable. Therefore, (D) is incorrect. Because a correct choice is provided, (E) is incorrect.

27. **(D)** *Verstehen* was the term Weber used to describe his method for analyzing a particular social phenomenon. (A) "Social view" is not a sociological term. (B) The looking-glass self is a concept made popular by Charles Horton Cooley, which refers to how the self is formed in response to others. (C) is incorrect. Symbolic interaction is the paradigm which views society as the product of individual's interactions. (E) is incorrect. Social statics is a term made popular by Herbert Spencer.

28. **(E)** The symbolic interaction perspective looks to individual interaction and interpretation to explain social behavior. In the example, individual lawyers for the prosecution and defense interpret each others actions and reactions. (A) is incorrect. The structural functionalist perspective views society on a macro level, looking not to individual interaction, but how society's parts fit together to maintain stability. (B) is incorrect. Social conflict perspective looks to the friction and conflict underlying society's institutions and groups in explaining particular phenomenon. (C) is incorrect. Ethnocentrism refers to judging of another culture, seeing yours as superior. (D) is incorrect. Socialization refers to the process by which an individual becomes human and acquires a "self." It is a process studied in sociology and does not refer to any of the three major perspectives, or paradigms, covered in sociology (functionalism; social conflict; symbolic interactionism).

29. **(D)** Institutional discrimination occurs when inequalities are built into institutions and disproportionately disadvantages an entire category of people based on nothing more than their group membership. Institutional discrimination is unintended and carried out by institutions, not individuals. (B) and (C) are incorrect as they include the incorrect statement II. A landlord's distaste for Latino applicants is a form of individual discrimination, where the intentional discriminatory behavior is carried out by an

individual. (A) is incorrect because it only includes one of the three correct responses. Because a correct answer is provided, (E) is incorrect.

30. **(C)**   The majority of welfare dollars go to children, who are the biggest group falling below the poverty line. (A) is incorrect. Statistics show that women who receive welfare do not have more children on the average than those who do not collect welfare. (B) Males have more difficulty getting public assistance and are not the primary recipients of aid. Less than five percent of those on welfare are males who are able to work. (D) is incorrect. Every year, about one-third of welfare recipients climb out of welfare, while that same number or more fall into welfare. (E) is incorrect, since a correct response has been provided.

31. **(C)**   Interviews with both blacks and whites suggest that blacks, more than whites, desire integrated neighborhoods. Blacks prefer to live in neighborhoods that are racially mixed, although most express a fear of being the first black family in a white neighborhood. (A) is incorrect, as blacks express the exact opposite preference. (B) and (D) are incorrect. Whites do not prefer to maintain a segregated system in terms of public accommodations and housing, although they did express a preference to live in all-white neighborhoods. In one survey, 25 percent of whites said they would move to a new neighborhood if more than one black family bought a house in the area. (E) A correct answer is provided, so (E) is incorrect.

32. **(C)**   Strain theory asserts that people commit crimes when their means for achievement are obstructed. According to this theory, all of us desire the "American Dream" but only some of us are put in positions to achieve that dream. The consequence is that those people blocked from achievement find illegitimate means to succeed. This theory, therefore, is best at explaining crime among the less advantaged. Committing robbery, according to this theory, suggests that a disadvantaged individual is stealing because he may acquire goods and possessions that we all desire. (A) is incorrect. Voyeurism is not a crime that reaps a material reward and is not necessarily committed by disadvantaged individuals. (B), (D), and (E) are incorrect for the same reasons. Smoking marijuana, jaywalking, and speeding are not usually done to reap a material reward, nor are they committed primarily by disadvantaged individuals.

33. **(C)**   Studies suggest that police take race and class cues into account in the arrest process. (A) is incorrect. No evidence suggests that

lower-class youth commit more dangerous crimes; rather they commit different crimes. While a dangerous crime like robbery is more often committed by lower-class individuals, other dangerous crimes, such as arson, are more likely to be committed by middle-class youth. (B) is incorrect. There are not more police in lower-class neighborhoods. Often there are less. Areas with high poverty values (i.e., middle-class neighborhoods) usually have the tax base to support a large police force. (D) and (E) are incorrect. Youth of all social classes are equally likely to commit crimes; they simply commit different types of crimes. Lower-class youth are only more likely to be arrested for the crimes they commit.

34. **(D)**   A role is a behavior expected of a certain status. The expected behaviors of a professor are to meet with her students and prepare lectures. (A) is incorrect. A master status is the central defining status. This example is not addressing the status of professors, but the roles associated with that status. (B) is incorrect. An ascribed status refers to a social position based on involuntary characteristics, such as age, sex, and race. (C) is incorrect. An achieved status is a social position based largely on one's own merit. This question asks for the obligations associated with a status, but doesn't ask which type of status. (B) and (C) refer to a type of status. (E) is incorrect. Impression management refers to the manipulation of one's role.

35. **(E)**   The generalized other is Mead's term for the cultural norms and values we use as references when evaluating ourselves. That the children are able to internalize these norms and values suggests they are capable of understanding another's position. (A) and (B) are incorrect as no such sociological terms exists. (C) The looking glass self concept comes from Cooley, Mead's predecessor, and refers to the process of forming our self on the basis of others' responses to us. (D) is incorrect. Verstehen means the developing of a subjective understanding of a particular social phenomenon. Mead did not popularize or expand on this term.

36. **(E)**   Social research is more difficult to perform than other forms of research for a variety of reasons. Firstly, objectivity is impossible because social researchers are studying the same species as themselves. Secondly, humans, as opposed to other animals, are self-aware and are capable of manipulating their behavior under study conditions. For example, an individual may give a researcher the answer she thinks is desired. Finally, operations performed on animals or molecules cannot be performed on humans for ethical reasons. (A), (B), and (D) are incorrect as they contain

only parts of the entire answer. (C) is incorrect. The methods of social research are no more advanced than other methods of research.

37. **(B)** A systematic sample is when the researcher selects every element for the sample. (A) is incorrect. A random sample simply means that every observation has an equal chance of being selected for the sample. Although this example is an illustration of a random sample, a systematic sample is the specific type of random sample. (C) is incorrect. A cluster sample is a sampling method used where the units are clustered together and selected in stages. (D) A stratified sample is one that is first divided into strata before the researcher randomly selects her cases. (E) is incorrect. All of the previous sampling methods are representative, meaning that the results can be generalized to a larger population. Non-representative implies that the sampling is not random.

38. **(D)** That education level has no bearing on whether or not someone uses condoms suggests that no relationship exists between these two variables. (A) and (B) are incorrect since they suggest education level influences condom use. If a correlation did exist between the two variables, we would see one increasing as the other decreases, or we would see them both increasing/decreasing together. Nothing in this example implies that a causal relationship exists between these two variables. (E) is incorrect. A spurious relationship is when a third variable is able to explain the movement of the other two. No third variable is brought into this example.

39. **(B)** Race is not a biological fact, but a social construction. The sociologist's interest in race, then, is how meaning and value are attached to differences, both real and perceived, between groups. (A) is incorrect because race is a social fact, not a biological fact. Biologically, there is no basis for a relationship between race and behavior. Stratification on the basis of race is actually one of the most recent forms of stratification; sex and age are the oldest. (C) and (D) are therefore incorrect. Because a correct answer is provided, (E) is incorrect.

40. **(D)** Cultural assimilation refers to how well a group has adopted the norms, values, customs, and language of the dominant group. Because the "Zorn" have completely done so, their cultural assimilation has been high. Secondary assimilation refers to how well integrated the group is on a macro institutional level; that is, how equal they are in terms of money and political representation. The "Zorn" have some political representation, but because inequality still exists, they are only moderately assimi-

lated. Primary structural assimilation refers to integration on a micro institutional level such as the family. In this example, neighborhoods are not well integrated and inter-marriage is remarkably low, so primary structural assimilation is low. Only (D) answers in the correct order. (A), (B), and (C) place the cultural assimilation as low, or only moderate, making these incorrect choices. (E) is incorrect because it characterizes primary structural assimilation as moderate, when it is actually very low.

41. **(E)** Women earn 60 percent of what men do for a variety of reasons. Firstly, bosses continue to see women as less capable than male workers and promote them less frequently. Secondly, jobs are titled differently depending on who fills it. The Equal Pay Act states that men and women filling the same position must be paid the same. Employers are getting around this by hiring a male as an "administrative assistant" and a woman as a "secretary." They are entitled to pay the "administrative assistant" more than the "secretary," in spite of the fact their job roles and tasks are the same. Finally, women are paid less because they often have less labor market experience. In the process of child-bearing and rearing, many women do not have continuous labor market experience, which enables employers to pay them less. Only answer (E) includes all of these reasons.

42. **(A)** An informal sanction is direct social pressure from those around us to conform. By scorning him, Tom's classmates are putting social pressure on him to come to class on time. (B) is incorrect. A formal sanction is pressure to conform that is enforced by a formal institution, such as the criminal justice system. (C) and (D) are incorrect. Norms are rules of behavior and values are ideals and goals. The other students scorning Tom is not an example of either of these concepts. (E) is incorrect since a correct response has been provided.

43. **(B)** Studies interviewing rapists suggest that the motive for rape is not the desire for sex, as one might think, but rather power and domination. Rapists are looking not for sex, but for control, which is evidenced by the fact that most are married or have sexual partners. The crimes of embezzlement, car theft, and jaywalking show motives other than power, such as financial reward and material gain.

44. **(B)** Mechanical solidarity is Durkheim's term for social bonds that are based on shared moral sentiments. Usually these types of bonds were found among people living in pre-industrial societies. (A) is incorrect. Organic solidarity is the term Durkheim used to describe the bonds

that unite members of industrialized nations. (C) and (D) are incorrect, as no such sociological terms exist. Because a correct answer is provided, (E) is incorrect.

45. **(C)**   The population of the study is the people who are the focus of the research; the group to whom you are trying to generalize. In this case, the researcher is trying to find out something about all college students. (A) is incorrect. The students only on her campus are not representative of all American students. (B) The students randomly chosen for a response are the actual study sample. (D) An individual student who was surveyed would be the unit of analysis, not the population. (E) All people between the ages of 18-21 are not necessarily the population because many people within this age range are not college students.

46. **(E)**   Two opposing views have dominated discussion concerning the inverse relationship between level of education and prejudice. It has long been noted that as the level of education increases, the level of prejudice decreases. One view suggests that as the level of education increases, individuals become more critical thinkers and no longer accept things at face value. The result is that they are less likely to endorse stereotypes because they become more tolerant. Another view, however, suggests that educated people are no less prejudiced, but are only more careful about revealing it. (B) includes only one of the correct responses, as does (C), therefore, they are both incorrect. (A) is incorrect. Evidence suggest that less educated people are more likely to be prejudice regardless of their level of contact with various racial/ethnic groups, thus, (D) is incorrect.

47. **(C)**   Rigid endogamy refers to marriage within one's only group. A caste system is a system of stratification where groups are strictly ranked on the basis of ethnic group. Marriage across these groups is unlawful and uncommon. (A) A stratification system can be based on a number of criteria, such as sex, age, or race, but in-group marriage is only a feature of stratification systems based on race, and sometimes age. (B) A class system is a stratification system based, at least partially, on achievement. While individuals of the same class generally do marry one another, it is not rigidly enforced and people marry outside their social class relatively frequently. (D) is incorrect. A polygamous society is one where individuals can marry more than one partner. This is not an issue in the current example. Since a correct answer is provided, (E) is incorrect.

48. **(E)**   Opponents to affirmative action argue that enhancing one group's opportunities is equivalent to reverse discrimination. Another point they argue is that such programs only help those minorities in a position to take advantage. Many jobs are available only to skilled workers and college graduates. The majority of minorities are not skilled or college educated; therefore, such programs do not help them. They are in greater need of programs that help them become skilled and educated so that they can eventually take advantage of opportunities available to them. Finally, opponents contend that minorities only suffer from such programs because they become labeled as an individual who got a job only as a hand-out. The result is that whites will feel as though their jobs are being unfairly taken by an unqualified minority, creating greater prejudice. Only choice (E) includes all three statements.

49. **(C)**   A subculture is a culture within a culture. This Irish-American community possesses its own unique culture while still operating within the larger American society. (A) is incorrect. A counterculture is a culture that rejects the larger society's norms and values (i.e., cults). The Irish-American subculture is not rejecting all that is American, but is instead adopting elements of both Irish culture and American culture. (B) Non-material culture refers to the non-material aspects of culture, such as norms and values, and is therefore irrelevant to this question. (D) and (E) are incorrect. Nothing from this example suggests that Irish-American subculture is either deviant or ethnocentric.

50. **(A)**   The defining characteristic of closed systems is rigid boundaries between classes. (B) is irrelevant because how closed or open a system is has nothing to do with immigration but with movement up and down in the stratification hierarchy. (C) is wrong because closed systems have clear, rigid, and impermeable boundaries. People may cross boundaries unnoticed in a closed system, but the boundaries are clear. (D) and (E) are incorrect because hereditary position and ascribed statuses are very important in determining class position in a closed system.

51. **(E)**   Ascribed statuses are those statuses which are involuntary and in no way relate to individual merit. Sex, race, and age are all involuntary, or unchosen, statuses. Only (E) includes all three. (A) and (D) are incorrect because while two ascribed statuses are included, the status of Olym-

pic athlete and pediatrician are at least partly voluntary, or achieved. (B) is incorrect for the same reason. Being a rabbi is a voluntary, achieved status. (C) While being female is ascribed, being married and pregnant are voluntary statuses.

52. **(B)**   The earliest arguments for why some ethnic groups seemed to be in better economic positions than others was rooted in Darwinism and the concept of "survival of the fittest." This perspective suggests that those possessing better genes would be more likely to survive and thrive, while those possessing flawed genes would suffer from poverty and misery. Other generations, those with flawed genes would die out. (A) is incorrect, as Darwinism did not include any ideas about how race and skin color would lead to extinction. (C) is also incorrect; Darwin talked specifically about genetics, not about culture. However, later theorists adapted his argument to culture. (D) Selective migration does explain a group's success upon migration. However, Darwin did not discuss these ideas. (E) is incorrect because a correct answer has been established.

53. **(B)**   Karl Marx referred to the owners of the means of production as the bourgeoisie. (D) The proletariat are the people who provide the labor necessary for the operation of the factories and other productive enterprises. (A), (C), and (E) are terms used to describe those in power, but were not used by Marx.

54. **(D)**   American Indians have the highest unemployment rate in the United States. On some reservations the rate soars to about 90 percent. (A) African-Americans and (C) Latinos have unemployment rates, on the average, double the rate of whites. This is referred to as the two-to-one rule. If white employment is at 7 percent, African-American and Latino unemployment usually hovers around 14 percent. The unemployment rate for (B) Asian-Americans is generally low, often lower than the rate of unemployment among whites.

55. **(B)**   Through the process of industrialization, the extended family declined as families needed to be more geographically mobile. The nuclear family was therefore deprived of support from the extended kin. (A) is incorrect. That children are viewed as an economic liability, as opposed to an economic benefit, was a result of industrialization. Large families are necessary for agricultural work, but not manufacturing work. As families became more mobile and were no longer involved in agricul-

ture, having many children became a burden rather than an asset. (C) Rather than the size of the nuclear family hindering geographic mobility, it enhances mobility. (D) is incorrect. That gender roles are less rigid than in other family forms is not necessarily a dysfunction. It may have positive effects, such as greater equality for women.

56. **(B)** Studies show that teacher perceptions greatly influence student performance. Students tend to perform to the level of expectations a teacher sets for them, whether high or low. A self-fulfilling prophecy occurs when students internalize their teacher's image of them, and in turn, conform to that image. Carol Gilligan's work using the concept of the looking glass has illustrated this process occurring in the classroom. The teacher is a mirror, or looking glass, reflecting an image of ourselves. Our self-image, then, is based on how others, including teachers, respond to us. (A) and (C) are incorrect since they state the opposite. (D) Rather than teachers influencing all of us equally, they respond to students differently and, therefore, have differing influences on them. (E) is incorrect, as it diminishes the role of the teacher in influencing student performance, as illustrated in Gilligan's work.

57. **(C)** In the last three decades, our economy has moved from producing goods to producing services. The service sector of the economy is the fastest-growing sector. As an employee of the twenty-first century, John will have the best luck finding a job in the growing service sector. Both the manufacturing sector (A) and the agricultural sector (B) have been declining over the last 30 years. (D) No such sector as the international sector exists. (E) Employment in the government sector in the twenty-first century is difficult to gauge. As administrations change, the role of the government expands and contracts.

58. **(C)** Karl Marx contended religion was the "opiate of the masses," as it allowed them to escape, if only temporarily, the miserable conditions they lived in. For the masses, the present was a hopeless, futile state of living. Through religion, they could focus on the after-life and the good things to come. (A) is incorrect; Marx focused on the role religion played in pacifying the masses, and addressed the power dynamics between the masses and the bourgeoisie. (B) Religion, for Marx, was not the center of all conflict. Conflict was the center of all social relations due to the incompatible interests between those who own the means of production (bourgeoisie) and those who do not (proletariat). (D) is incorrect since it includes the incorrect statement II. (E) is incorrect since it includes statements I and II, which are incorrect.

59. **(D)** Following WWII, movement to the suburbs became popular. This movement was made possible by improvements in transportation. Not only did public transportation become more widespread, but automobiles became affordable to the middle and working classes. (A) The decrease in birth rate is unrelated to the growth of the suburbs and actually preceded suburban growth. (B) Decline in agriculture also preceded suburban growth and, instead, is related to urban growth. (C) is incorrect. During the expansion of suburbs, rural areas were declining in population, not increasing. (E) is incorrect since a correct answer has been provided.

60. **(D)** Over-urbanization is when the population grows too quickly for the infrastructure to handle. Housing and jobs become difficult to find and the city is unable to absorb the new population. (A) Industrialization refers to the technological development of a country. This example is only discussing an urban area. (B) Gentrification is when a rundown section of the city has been repaired and has become attractive to a middle-class population. This process is independent to the growth of a city's population. (C) is incorrect as under-urbanization is the exact opposite of what is occurring in this example. (E) is incorrect as a correct answer has been provided.

61. **(B)** Information on illegal aliens is very difficult to obtain since keeping anonymous is so important for remaining in the country. Since information on the elderly, prisoners, and students are all included in the census, all other answer choices are incorrect.

62. **(E)** Normative theory of prejudice states that individuals become prejudiced when such attitudes are so ingrained in their society's norms and values that they get passed on from generation to generation without question. (A) is incorrect. Power-conflict theory of prejudice focuses on the power dynamics between those who are prejudiced and those who are prejudiced against. (B) and (D) are both incorrect. Both see prejudice as the result of frustration. The majority is frustrated, perhaps due to current economic hardship, and they take this frustration out on an alternative target, the scapegoat. Very often the alternative target is a minority group. (C) is incorrect. Authoritarian-personality theory of prejudice sees prejudice as stemming from certain personality characteristics. Individuals who possess such traits as conformity and obedience are more likely to be prejudiced than those who do not.

63. **(B)** Those groups who would maintain the sociological content of the American population were favored. Simply put, those who could easily

assimilate were given preference to those who physically and culturally were different from the majority. (A) is incorrect. From the 1960s on, immigration policy changed so that those possessing the most skills and highest education were favored over the unskilled and uneducated. (D) While certain immigration acts prohibiting the entrance of Chinese were put into effect around the turn of the century, such acts are different from the quota system. (E) is incorrect, as a correct answer is provided.

64. **(A)** Horizontal mobility is the movement of an individual horizontally. Since Sue is moving from one elite professorial position to another, she is neither moving up nor down. (B) is incorrect. Vertical mobility refers to movement of an individual in either direction. If Sue had gotten a job as president of an elite university, she would be vertically mobile. (C) Intergenerational mobility is movement across generations. We are only focusing on one generation in this example. (D) Status mobility is not a sociological term. (E) is incorrect since a correct answer is provided.

65. **(D)** Affirmative action programs attempt to address institutional discrimination. Prejudice becomes built into institutions and disproportionately disadvantages minorities. Institutional discrimination is covert and difficult to detect. Affirmative action policies have attacked workplaces that allow no other languages besides English to be spoken. Another form of institutional discrimination which has been addressed by affirmative action is policies that prevent women from taking time off to have a baby. In many workplaces women who left to have a baby were not guaranteed their job back upon their return. Affirmative action policies have also addressed discriminatory lending policies, making certain that individuals of minority backgrounds are given opportunities to buy homes and businesses. Only (D) includes all responses. (C) is incorrect. Landlords who overtly refuse to rent to minorities do not fall under "institutional discrimination," but "individual discrimination."

66. **(C)** Regardless of the fact that we are a secular society, religion is in no way losing its role in society. Ninety-four percent of Americans report believing in God, and religion remains a central institution in virtually every culture on earth. (A) is incorrect as it states nearly the opposite. The role of religion is not diminishing. (B) While the role of other institutions, such as government and education have taken over some of the functions religion once filled, the functions they fill are mundane (profane), and ones we in no way hold as sacred. (D) is incorrect. Religion continues to be a central feature of all classes, races, and genders. (E) is incorrect since a correct response is provided.

67. **(B)** Tracking is the assignment of students to different types of educational programs. Larry is being placed in a high math "track" and is exposed to a different type of education program than those individuals placed into the medium or low math "track." (A) is incorrect. A stratification system is a system of structured inequality and influences the opportunities of everyone in the society, not just the people in the class. (C) is incorrect because a tiered system has no sociological meaning. (D) is incorrect. A bureaucratic system is a system rationally designed to perform complex tasks efficiently. This does not have relevance to the placement of Larry in a high math "track." (E) is incorrect since a correct answer has been provided.

68. **(D)** Multinational corporations establish subsidiaries in other countries primarily to access a cheap labor supply and decrease their taxes. By moving to developing countries, companies can find a pliant labor supply who will work at a fraction of the cost of American workers. (A) and (B) are both incorrect. Although these can also be benefits to moving a company abroad, they are not the primary reasons. Many companies are not in need of the available natural resources, they are in need of the cheap labor and taxes. (C) is incorrect. Corporations are not inherently altruistic, and do not seek to help develop the countries where they establish subsidiaries. To the contrary, they often relocate to such areas because they are less developed. (E) is incorrect since a correct answer is provided.

69. **(D)** Civil religion is a quasi-religious loyalty binding individuals in a secular state. The citizen's loyalties are to the state, rather than to a specific religion. (A) is incorrect. There is no religion specifically endorsed by the government. Instead, we are made up of a myriad of religions. (B) Secularization refers to the decline in importance of the supernatural and the sacred. Civil religion is a binding force in a largely secular society. The teacher is not teaching the students about the lack of importance of religion in American society. He is actually teaching that religion, civil religion, is very important. The United States economic system is not socialism, but capitalism. (E) is incorrect since a correct response is provided.

70. **(A)** Although the first suburbanites were predominately white and wealthy, in the last four decades moving to the suburbs has come within the reach of middle- and working-class people. Bob is probably poor since he has been unable to move to the suburbs. Only (A) includes the status of being poor. (B), (C), (D), and (E) state that Bob is either middle or working class, which implies he should be able to move to the suburbs if he so chooses.

71. **(C)** Gentrification is when a rundown section of a city has been repaired and revitalized and has become attractive to a middle-class population. (A) Industrialization refers to the technological development of a country. This example refers not to technological development of a country, but to the revitalization of a small urban area within a larger city. (B) Over-urbanization is when an urban area has developed more quickly than the infrastructure is able to handle. (D) is incorrect. Suburbanization is the movement of people to areas surrounding the urban region. This example is discussing the revitalization of the urban areas, not the areas surrounding it. (E) Centralization has no sociological significance.

72. **(C)** An ideology of racism, which states that some races are innately superior to others, has been used to justify stratification systems based on race. If people of a certain race are unequal, it is because they are innately inferior. (A) and (D) are incorrect since they include statement I. There is no biological link between race and personality traits. If such behavioral differences do occur, it is the result of social, not biological forces. (B) is incorrect. Race stratification is not synonymous with slavery. Enslavement on the basis of race is actually quite recent. Historically, individuals have been enslaved on the basis of characteristics other than race, such as religion, and sex. Since a correct response has been provided, choice (E) is incorrect.

73. **(D)** The "culture of poverty" concept seeks to explain poverty as stemming not from structural forces, but cultural forces. (A), (B), and (C) all use a cultural argument to explain poverty, seeing it as stemming from weaknesses inherent to certain cultures. Such weaknesses include a present-time orientation, feeling of victimization, and laziness. Only (D) discusses larger social forces that prevent people from becoming economically independent.

74. **(A)** The authoritarian-personality theory of aggression explains prejudice as residing in individuals who carry a particular personality trait (extreme conformity, obedience to high authority). This theory, then, is only able to explain prejudice in those few people who possess such personality configurations (i.e., Hitler). It is unable to explain the majority of the people who show some prejudices but do not possess such a personality. (B) is incorrect. The normative theory of prejudice best explains the transmission of prejudice across generations because it focuses on how prejudiced norms and values become embedded in our everyday lives. (C) Power-conflict is best able to explain the benefits a majority receives from

subjugating a minority. (D) is incorrect. Authoritarian-personality looks for prejudice in a few, while (D) is addressing the prejudices we all carry. (E) is incorrect, as a correct answer has been provided.

75. **(B)**   Adults in pre-industrial societies generally view marriage as an economic arrangement. Marriage in these societies is typically an alliance made by two extended families. Uniting on the basis of romantic love is a relatively recent phenomenon, as well as a Western phenomenon, thus, (A) is incorrect. (C) is incorrect. In most pre-industrial societies marriage is not viewed as a polygamous relationship. This type of marriage is defined by the uniting of three or more persons. (D) includes the incorrect statement II, and is therefore incorrect. Because a correct response is provided, (E) is incorrect.

76. **(D)**   Women are more likely to sustain injuries in a family dispute, although men and women are equally likely to get killed in family arguments. Studies suggest that abusers, both men and women, are often abuse victims themselves. Studies also show that women who are killed are very often the victim of their spouse, ex-spouse, or sexual partner. Only (D) includes all three statements. (A) is incorrect. Abusers fall into all social classes and races. No class, race, or religion is free from domestic violence. (E) is incorrect since a correct answer is provided.

77. **(D)**   Individuals who have a high level of autonomy in their jobs report high satisfaction levels. They feel as if they have a choice in the decisions they make, and that their bosses trust them. (A) is incorrect. Those possessing a lot of autonomy hold all sorts of career positions, some of which are high paying and some of which aren't. (B) Interestingly, those with a lot of autonomy don't feel unchallenged. They are able to create and design many of their own tasks. (C) is incorrect as it states the exact opposite. (E) is incorrect since a correct answer is provided.

78. **(A)**   Social class is the biggest predictor of voting behavior, with the higher classes more likely to vote than the lower classes. Age is another strong correlate to voting behavior, with elderly people more likely to vote than the young. In example (A) the individual is both young and of a lower social class, making her less likely to vote than the individuals in the remaining examples. The individuals in examples (B), (C), and (D) are all middle or upper-middle class, making them more likely to vote than the individual in example (A). (E) is incorrect. Although not of a high social class, the individual in example (E) is of a higher social class than individual (A), and is also older.

79. **(E)** Fertility, mortality, and migration all affect a society's population. Fertility is the incidence of childbearing in a society's population. Mortality is the incidence of death in a society's population. Migration is the movement of people into and out of a specified territory. Only these three factors affect the net increase/decrease of a population. (A), (B), and (C), which only include one of the three correct responses, are incorrect. (D) is incorrect. Urbanization refers to the concentration of humanity into cities and is unrelated to the net increase/decrease of population.

80. **(E)** None of the statements are correct. An age-sex population pyramid is a graphic representation of the age and sex of the population. Rather than having a pictorial representation that is heavy at the top and bottom, in the United States, the middle of the age-sex pyramid is thickest (ages 20-39). The Mexican representation is very heavy at the bottom (0-19) and gets increasingly thinner as age increases. Across all age groups in all societies, women outlive men.

81. **(D)** Demographers use the term fecundity to explain a woman's potential number of children. The average childbearing years are between the ages of 15-44. The number of children a woman can have during these years is referred to as fecundity. (B) is incorrect as it is the birth rate. (C) is incorrect as it is the sex ratio. Because a correct answer is provided, (E) is incorrect.

82. **(A)** Attempts to count the homeless have been unsuccessful because a number of homeless individuals have escaped detection, which has resulted in a drastic underestimation of who really is homeless. (B) is the opposite response and suggests we may overestimate the number of homeless. (C) For the majority, living on the street was not a choice, but the outcome of economic and social problems. Because previous choices have been illustrated as faulty, (E) is incorrect.

83. **(C)** Feminism does not hold that women are innately superior to men. That is a sexist notion, not a feminist one. (A), (B), and (D) are all goals of the feminist movement. Feminists would like to see a broader spectrum of roles for women. Allowing women to have jurisdiction over their own bodies in terms of sexuality and reproduction is another goal, as is eliminating violence against women. Since a correct answer is provided, (E) is incorrect.

84. **(B)** Vertical mobility refers to movement within the social system where the individual can move up or down. Mark is moving from an office

manager down to a position of a secretary. (A) Horizontal mobility refers to horizontal mobility in the system. If Mark would have found another job as an office manager, he would be experiencing horizontal mobility. (C) Intergenerational mobility is the movement of individuals across generations, for example, comparing your own position with your father's position. (D) Status mobility has no sociological meaning. (E) is incorrect since a correct response has been provided.

85. **(D)**   Sociologists who study religion are interested in religion as a social institution. Sociologists look at characteristics of certain religions as well as characteristics of the individuals making up these institutions. (A), (B), and (C) are all incorrect. The sociology of religion does not address questions of the supernatural or the existence of God. Religion deals with ideas that neither common sense nor science can verify or disprove. Because a correct answer is provided, (E) is incorrect.

86. **(D)**   Twenty-five percent of white single mothers fall below the poverty line, and 50+ percent of Latino and African-American single mothers fall below the poverty line. Molly, as a single parent with two children, has a fairly good chance of being poor, or near poverty. (A) and (B) are incorrect. Single mothers live in an array of family arrangements— with parents, grandparents, alone, with a partner, etc. (C) Molly may or may not live in an urban area. Poverty affects individuals living in urban areas, rural areas, and suburban areas.

87. **(B)**   Black male youth have among the highest unemployment rates in the United States, double that of their white male counterparts. (A) and (D) are incorrect. Black women and men both have astronomical unemployment rates, although women and men over 50 are less likely to be unemployed than young black men. (C) Although white females have higher unemployment rates than white males, they are lower than young black males'. (E) White males under 50 have the lowest unemployment rates of the preceding groups.

88. **(B)**   A large share of the people eligible to vote in the United States do not. This pattern of voter apathy has been increasing over the last century to the point that the United States has nearly the lowest rate of voting in the democratic world. Fewer than 60 percent of eligible voters turned out for the 1992 election. (A) is incorrect as it states nearly the opposite. (C) is incorrect. People of lower social classes are actually less likely to vote due to feelings of alienation and powerlessness. (D) is incor-

rect. The likelihood of the elderly voting in the United States is high. People over 65 are twice as likely to vote as young adults. (E) is incorrect since a correct answer has been provided.

89. **(B)**   Due to improvements in nutrition and health care across the globe, the death rate has declined in all countries. This has been responsible for a boom in the population because people are no longer dying at such young ages. (A), (D), and (E) are incorrect as they include statements I and II. The birth rate has not increased dramatically, and in some areas has decreased with the advent of birth control. However, the decrease in birth rate has not been marked enough to offset the increase in life expectancy. Additionally, there is no evidence to suggest that people from developing countries engage in sex more frequently. (C) is incorrect. It does not make sense, logically, that a sharp increase in both death and birth rates would result in a population boom.

90. **(A)**   Pull factors refer to the reasons one migrates to a particular area. Leon is moving to Colorado because he has a good job and there are more potential dating partners. (B) is incorrect. Push factors refer to the reasons one wants to leave a certain area. There is no evidence to suggest from this example that Leon is leaving Alabama for a reason. He is not being pushed out. (C) and (D) are incorrect since these terms have no real sociological meaning. (E) is incorrect since a correct answer is provided.

91. **(C)**   Originally, those who moved to the suburbs were well-to-do and mostly white. Following World War II, when the economy boomed and automobiles became within reach of average Americans, suburban areas boomed. Today, suburbanites are as diverse as urbanites. (A) is incorrect. Early suburbanites were upper-middle class, however today, suburban living is within the reach of most Americans. (B) and (D) are incorrect. While suburbanites are more diverse than they were 50 years ago, suburbanites today are not mostly made up of minorities and working class. They are of diverse classes and ethnic backgrounds. (E) is incorrect since a correct response has been provided.

92. **(D)**   A decline in public aid, inexpensive housing, and in the need for unskilled labor have all contributed to the increased homeless rate. The economy has moved from producing goods to producing services which has had the negative impact of a declining need for unskilled workers. This, coupled with cutbacks in aid and inexpensive housing during the Reagan administration, have led to an increase in homelessness. Only (D)

includes all three explanations. (C) is incorrect. Problems of drug and alcohol abuse do not seem to be increasing, and though sometimes correlated to homelessness, have not caused the increase. Instead, social structural, not individual, forces explain why homelessness has increased in recent years.

93. **(B)** The increase in single-parent families is the result of more women having children out-of-wedlock. This trend is apparent across all social classes and groups of women. (A) is incorrect. Although the divorce rate has increased and is a contributing factor to the increased number of single-parent households, it is not the main cause. (C) and (D) are incorrect as they don't make logical sense. The social pressure to get married once pregnant implies that families are two-parent. The decrease in extended families has no direct bearing on whether a family is headed by one or two people. (E) is incorrect because a correct answer is provided.

94. **(D)** Studies show that most people marry within their social class background and educational background, and even more marry within their race. Class, education, and race appear to be more important than similar personality characteristics when looking at potential marriage partners, as few people marry someone with a similar personality configuration. Only (D) includes the first three statements.

95. **(D)** The sacred, referring to that which is defined as inspiring a sense of awe, reverence, and even fear, according to Durkheim, symbolically represents society. The sacred, or "forbidden," is set apart from the profane, or "mundane." Although Jesus (A), the family (B), and one's parents (C) may be designated as sacred entities, only society, according to Durkheim, is the symbolic representation of all that is sacred. (E) is incorrect since a correct answer is provided.

96. **(D)** Push factors of migration refer to the reasons an individual leaves a certain area. The cold weather, losing a job, and experiencing religious persecution are all reasons an individual would want to leave an area. Pull factors refer to the reasons an individual is pulled to a certain location; why they desire to live in a particular place. (A), (B), and (C) all include pull factors of warm climate, good schools, and a new job. (E) is incorrect since a correct answer has been provided.

97. **(B)** Originally, people who moved to the suburbs were wealthy and largely white. This was because transportation was poor and only

those with financial resources could afford the expense of trains and auto-mobiles. As public transportation improved, more classes and races of people had access to the suburbs. (A) and (C) are therefore incorrect. (D) is incorrect. Suburban areas are those immediately surrounding the urban centers. Agricultural workers were living in rural areas, not suburban areas. (E) is incorrect since a correct response has been provided.

98. **(D)**   Since the 1950s, urban decentralization has been taking place where families are relocating in the suburbs. But this has not always been without problems. Suburbs, too, have become very populated and experienced decay. This has resulted in a more recent move to rural areas. (A) is incorrect. No evidence suggests that Americans have been moving out of the country as a result of urban and suburban decay. (B) is incorrect. The movement has not been to the snow-belt, but out of the snow-belt and into the sun-belt. While in 1940, 60 percent of the United States population lived in the snow-belt region, by 1975, almost 60 percent of the United States population lived in the sun-belt region. (C) As suburban and urban populations began to look more alike and suburban areas are afflicted with the same types of problems as urban areas, suburbanites have started to move back to the urban center. Urban revitalization programs have attempted to promote such a move by investing money with the goal of revitalizing cities. (E) is incorrect since a correct answer is provided.

99. **(D)**   Pluralism is when an ethnic minority group attempts to maintain their own distinctive culture, even though they live in a larger society that is sometimes at odds with their beliefs, norms, and values. (D) illustrates that the three ethnic groups (A, B, and C) maintain their uniqueness and do not change during contact with other groups. (A) is incorrect as it shows a pattern of assimilation. The ethnic groups take on the characteristics of the dominant one ("B and C become like A"). (B) illustrates a pattern of amalgamation/fusion where the groups that come into contact with one another blend together to form an entirely new product. (C) is incorrect as it depicts no discernible pattern of ethnic relations. (E) is incorrect since a correct answer choice is provided.

100. **(B)**   The extended family is a family unit that includes not only parents and their children, but other kin as well. This family form declined during industrialization because a small family was more functional in a changing economy. As the agricultural sector declined and manufacturing increased, families were forced to move where work was available. This often meant moving to smaller residences in cities. (A) is incorrect. Living

in a small residence was not necessarily preferred to living in a house. In many instances, it was a necessity. (C) and (D) are incorrect. Economic development did not necessarily mean families became financially independent and no longer needed the extended relatives for support. The increased number of non-kin relatives was an effect of the decline in extended families.

▼
PRACTICE
TEST 2

Bobby
724
622
1311

CLEP INTRODUCTORY SOCIOLOGY
Test 2

(Answer sheets appear in the back of this book.)

TIME: 90 Minutes
100 Questions

DIRECTIONS: Each of the questions or incomplete statements below is followed by five possible answers or completions. Select the best choice in each case and fill in the corresponding oval on the answer sheet.

1. Which of the following theorists created three categories of suicide: egoistic, altruistic, and anomic?

    (A) Max Weber   (D) Talcott Parsons

    (B) Emile Durkheim   (E) Auguste Comte

    (C) Karl Marx

2. Louise took five exams in her Introductory Sociology course. Her grades were 93, 75, 83, 88, and 81. What was her mean score for the semester?

    (A) 84   (D) 79

    (B) 83   (E) 89

    (C) 86

3. According to the theory of the demographic transition, the final stage in the transition process results in

    (A) high birth rates and high death rates.

    (B) high birth rates and low death rates.

1 (C) low birth rates and high death rates.

(D) low birth rates and low death rates.

(E) changes in agricultural output.

4. When new groups enter a society and experience high rates of inter-marriage with members of the host society, the new group will most likely go through which of the following processes?

(A) Separatism

(D) Segregation

(B) Amalgamation

(E) Multiculturalism

(C) Cultural pluralism

5. In Karl Marx's theory of social class in industrial capitalist societies, who owns the means of production?

(A) The bourgeoisie

(B) The proletariat

(C) The intellectual elite

(D) W.A.S.P.s

(E) Members of the Fortune 500

6. When a society has a norm which permits a man to have more than one wife at the same time, this is called the norm of

(A) monogamy.

(D) polygyny.

(B) serial monogamy.

(E) polyandry.

(C) polygamy.

7. The concepts of id, ego, and superego are associated with which of the following theorists?

(A) Piaget

(D) Cooley

(B) Kohlberg

(E) Freud

(C) Mead

8. Four American corporations produce approximately 80 percent of the world's light bulbs. This is an example of

135

(A) monopoly.

(D) oligopoly.

⁎(B) conglomerates.

(E) economic diversification.

(C) economic elite.

9. Howard is a college student who has a final examination tomorrow in Sociology 101. He must study as best he can to prepare for the exam. He has just received a phone call from his boss at the restaurant where he works part-time to help pay his college expenses. His boss tells him he must come to work immediately because a fellow worker has just called in sick. The sociological circumstance Howard is confronting is most accurately called

(A) role conflict.

(D) cognitive dissonance.

(B) role strain.

(E) emotional distress.

(C) trauma.

10. A social movement that attempts to modify the workings of society without making drastic changes in the society is called a(n)

(A) expressive movement.

(D) mob.

⁎(B) reform movement.

(E) radical movement.

(C) revolutionary movement.

11. Jose and Maria met, fell in love, and decided to marry. They are both Catholic and of Puerto Rican ancestry. Their marriage illustrates which of the following?

(A) The norm of exogamy

(B) The norm of endogamy

(C) Arranged marriages

(D) The stimulus-value-role theory

(E) Polyandrous marriages

12. Which of the following theorists argued that religion should be viewed as "the opiate of the masses"?

(A) Max Weber

(D) Emile Durkheim

(B) Ferdinand Tonnies

⁎(E) Karl Marx

(C) Sigmund Freud

13. The Islamic religion is based on

    (A) animism.   (D) theism.

    (B) monotheism.   (E) atheism.

    (C) polytheism.

14. Many school systems place students in classes based on their ability, social class, or other characteristics. This is called

    (A) testing out.

    (B) latent functions of education.

    (C) manifest functions of education.

    (D) tracking.

    (E) biased placement.

15. The idea that we should continue to follow the norms and laws of society because that is what we have always done is an illustration of

    (A) legal-rational authority.   (D) court precedent.

    (B) traditional authority.   (E) a system of sanctions.

    (C) charismatic authority.

16. Most economic systems in the world may be classified as

    (A) capitalist.   (D) laissez-faire economies.

    (B) socialist.   (E) communist economies.

    (C) mixed economies.

17. All of the following characteristics are elements of a totalitarian government EXCEPT

    (A) government control of the media.

    (B) government control of the military.

    (C) government control of the educational system.

    (D) an ideology which legitimates the current state.

    (E) several political parties.

18. The attempt by special interest groups to influence governmental policy is called

    (A) bribery.

    (D) lobbying.

    (B) illegal behavior.

    (E) deviant behavior.

    (C) white-collar crime.

19. When sociologists speak of the major social institutions, they usually refer to all of the following EXCEPT

    (A) family.

    (D) government.

    (B) economy.

    (E) education.

    (C) media.

20. Homeostasis, the integration of its parts, and the stability of social systems are all elements of which sociological theory?

    (A) Functionalist

    (D) Ethnomethodology

    (B) Conflict

    (E) Dramaturgy

    (C) Symbolic interactionist

21. A characteristic that can change from individual to individual or group to group is called a(n)

    (A) concept.

    (D) variable.

    (B) symbol.

    (E) experiment.

    (C) hypothesis.

22. The research method that follows a group of subjects over a period of time is called a(n)

    (A) cross-sectional study.

    (D) participant observation.

    (B) longitudinal study.

    (E) survey.

    (C) open-ended interview.

23. When one makes a judgment about other societies based upon the values and beliefs of one's own society, this is called

    (A) prejudice.

    (B) discrimination.

(C) bias.

(D) cultural shock.

(E) ethnocentrism.

24. Jewish Americans, police officers, and college students could all be characterized as

(A) countercultures.

(D) racial groups.

(B) subcultures.

(E) social classes.

(C) ethnic groups.

25. W. I. Thomas coined the phrase "definition of the situation." Thomas meant that when people define a situation as real, it becomes real in its consequences. This concept is most closely associated with which sociological theory?

(A) Functionalist

(D) Social exchange

(B) Conflict

(E) Dramaturgy

(C) Symbolic interactionist

26. Primary groups have all of the following characteristics EXCEPT

(A) a small number of members.

(B) they last for a long time.

(C) a limited knowledge of other members of the group.

(D) intimate communication.

(E) All of the above are characteristics of primary groups.

27. According to Max Weber's model of bureaucracy, all of the following are characteristics of a bureaucracy EXCEPT

(A) a fixed set of rules and regulations.

(B) power is distributed hierarchically.

(C) employment is based on the qualifications of the applicants.

(D) rules are to be meted out impartially.

(E) All of the above are characteristics of bureaucracies.

28. What term do sociologists use to describe the condition when a society no longer provides guidelines for behavior, and there exists a state of normlessness?

    (A) Alienation

    (D) Anomie

    (B) Fatalism

    (E) Innovation

    (C) Cognitive dissonance

29. Primary deviance and secondary deviance are concepts related to which of the following theories of deviance?

    (A) Labeling theory

    (D) Neutralization theory

    (B) Differential association

    (E) Strain theory

    (C) Control theory

30. With respect to gender roles, most sociologists would argue that gender role differences are largely a result of

    (A) biology.

    (D) the Oedipus complex.

    (B) individual psychology.

    (E) sociobiology.

    (C) socialization.

31. Thomas Malthus was most influential in the study of which area of specialization?

    (A) Urban problems

    (D) Politics

    (B) Population

    (E) Education

    (C) Economic problems

32. Tonnies, in his study of communities, argued that communities where relationships are personal and intimate may be called

    (A) *gemeinschaft.*

    (D) modern.

    (B) *gesellschaft.*

    (E) industrialized.

    (C) urban.

33. All of the following are theories of urban development EXCEPT

    (A) concentric zone theory.

(B) sector theory.

(C) multiple-nuclei theory.

(D) assimilation theory.

(E) All of the above are theories of urban development.

34. The process by which ideas and technology move from one culture to another is called

(A) invasion.   (D) cultural contact.

(B) acculturation.   (E) diffusion.

(C) evolution.

35. The idea that societies undergo gradual and continuous change from simple to more complex societies is most closely associated with

(A) functionalist theory.   (D) interactionist theory.

(B) conflict theory.   (E) revolution.

(C) evolutionary theory.

36. Concepts such as exploitation, inequality, and power relationship are most clearly associated with which sociological theory?

(A) Functionalist   (D) Evolutionary

(B) Conflict   (E) Dramaturgical

(C) Interactionist

37. At its most encompassing level, the "sociological imagination" links individual experiences to

(A) psychological predispositions.

(B) family background.

(C) forces in the larger society.

(D) racial identity.

(E) population patterns.

38. The American university most closely associated with the study of urban society and urban communities is

(A) Harvard University.

(B) the University of Chicago.

(C) the University of North Carolina.

(D) the University of Pennsylvania.

(E) New York University.

39. The play stage, game stage, and the concept of the generalized other is associated with the work of

(A) Sigmund Freud.   (D) Erik Erikson.

(B) George Herbert Mead.   (E) Daniel Levinson.

(C) Charles Horton Cooley.

40. The division of society into status positions is called

(A) stratification.   (D) the power elite.

(B) social mobility.   (E) social evaluation.

(C) status inconsistency.

41. Martin decides to change his job. He leaves his position as a research biologist and becomes a professor of biology at a nearby university. Both positions command the same salary and approximately the same degree of respect. Martin has experienced

(A) upward mobility.   (D) status inconsistency.

(B) downward mobility.   (E) intergenerational mobility.

(C) horizontal mobility.

42. Intragenerational mobility

(A) is the same as intergenerational change.

(B) is a problem because of status inconsistency.

(C) always results in upward mobility.

(D) is a product of one's family wealth.

(E) is a change in social position within one's lifetime.

43. The belief that one should judge other cultures within the context of that culture, not by comparing it to one's own culture, is called

    (A) ethnocentrism.

    (B) cultural pluralism.

    (C) culture relativism.

    (D) anthropology.

    (E) sociology.

44. The person whose work is most clearly associated with conflict theory is

    (A) Sigmund Freud.

    (B) Talcott Parsons.

    (C) Robert Merton.

    (D) Karl Marx.

    (E) George Herbert Mead.

45. The person who originally coined the word "sociology" was

    (A) Karl Marx.

    (B) Max Weber.

    (C) Emile Durkheim.

    (D) Auguste Comte.

    (E) Ferdinand Tonnies.

46. Another term for annihilation is

    (A) expulsion.

    (B) genocide.

    (C) assimilation.

    (D) amalgamation.

    (E) segregation.

47. One of the characteristics of a caste system is that it is based on

    (A) achieved status.

    (B) ascribed status.

    (C) intergenerational mobility.

    (D) intragenerational mobility.

    (E) None of the above are characteristics of a caste system.

48. C. Wright Mills' concept of the "power elite" included all of the following groups EXCEPT the

    (A) military elite.

(B) economic elite.

(C) political elite.

(D) media elite.

(E) All of the above were included in his concept.

49. The respect and approval we receive from other members of our group is referred to by sociologists as

(A) power.

(D) prestige.

(B) influence.

(E) authority.

(C) social class.

50. Given how people in the United States tend to rank occupations in terms of prestige, which of the following occupations would likely be given the lowest prestige ranking by people in the United States?

(A) Sociologist

(D) Police officer

(B) Dental assistant

(E) Bellhop

(C) Auto mechanic

51. Since World War II, which group has had the greatest increase in labor force participation rates?

(A) Teenagers

(D) African Americans

(B) Men

(E) Latino Americans

(C) Women

52. If 50 percent of the population is over 35 years of age, and 50 percent of the population is 35 years of age, the age 35 represents the country's _____ age.

    (A) mean

    (D) average

    (B) median

    (E) None of the above.

    (C) mode

53. Sociology first developed as a distinct discipline in the _____ century.

    (A) sixteenth

    (D) nineteenth

    (B) seventeenth

    (E) twentieth

    (C) eighteenth

54. According to Max Weber, the factors that determine social class position include all of the following EXCEPT

    (A) intelligence.

    (B) economic position.

    (C) social status.

    (D) political power.

    (E) All of the above determine class position.

55. The social class that is characterized by "old money," or substantial inherited wealth, is the

    (A) upper class.

    (D) working class.

    (B) upper-middle class.

    (E) lower class.

    (C) lower-middle class.

56. In which of the following societies is social mobility more likely to occur?

   (A) Caste system

   (B) Estate system

   (C) Class system

   (D) Systems based upon ascribed status

   (E) Tradition-based systems

57. Social class influences all of the following EXCEPT

   (A) educational attainment.   (D) recreational activities.

   (B) child rearing strategies.   (E) All of the above.

   (C) labor force participation.

58. The belief that men are superior and should be in control in the family and in society is called

   (A) patriarchy.   (D) patrilocal.

   (B) matriarchy.   (E) paternal.

   (C) patrilineal.

59. According to the conflict perspective, gender role differences continue to exist in modern industrial societies primarily because males

   (A) are smarter than females.

   (B) are physically stronger than females.

   (C) have a subconscious fear that females are really stronger than they are.

   (D) envy females' ability to bear children.

   (E) control the power structures in society.

60. Data indicate that on average, women working approximately the same occupations as men earn ____ percent of what men earn.

   (A) 50   (D) 80

   (B) 60   (E) 90

   (C) 70

61. A group of people who share certain physical and/or cultural characteristics, and who are victims of prejudice and discrimination are called a(n)

   (A) ethnic group.   (D) minority group.

   (B) racial group.   (E) marginal group.

   (C) majority group.

62. In Robert Merton's analysis of racial prejudice and discrimination, which of the following is not one of his "types"?

   (A) Unprejudiced nondiscriminator

   (B) Unprejudiced discriminator

   (C) Prejudiced nondiscriminator

   (D) Prejudiced discriminator

   (E) All of the above are included in Merton's analysis.

63. An Italian-American who speaks Italian in the home, and continues to follow some traditional Italian customs and traditions illustrates which of the following?

   (A) Assimilation   (D) Cultural pluralism

   (B) Anglo-conformity   (E) Subjugation

   (C) The melting pot

64. All of the following are functions of the family EXCEPT

    (A) regulating sexual behavior.

    (B) socializing children.

    (C) determining social status.

    (D) offering affection and companionship.

    (E) All of the above are functions of the family.

65. All of the following are contemporary trends in United States family patterns EXCEPT a(n)

    (A) increase in premarital sex.

    (B) increase in working wives/mothers.

    (C) decline in family size.

    (D) increase in the number of single-parent families.

    (E) increase in the average number of children per family.

66. Millenarian religious movements

    (A) are a product of Western culture.

    (B) are more spiritual than other types of religious movements.

    (C) predict the world will come to an end.

    (D) exist only in pre-industrial societies.

    (E) are similar to reform movements.

67. Secularization is the process by which people are

    (A) influenced by religious beliefs.

    (B) less influenced by religious beliefs.

    (C) searching for religious revelations.

    (D) returning to traditional ethical and moral beliefs.

    (E) seeking new religious interpretations.

68. According to functionalist theory, all of the following are functions of educational institutions EXCEPT

    (A) teaching academic skills.

(B) preparing young people for social change.

(C) socialization of the young.

(D) creating future citizens.

(E) providing child care.

69. The scientific study of population is called

(A) anthropology.   (D) fecundity.

(B) sociology.   (E) geography.

(C) demography.

70. An ideology that legitimates the subordination of women is called

(A) prejudice.   (D) sexism.

(B) racism.   (E) ethnocentrism.

(C) discrimination.

71. The sociological theory that uses the analogy of individuals as actors who may portray many different roles is called _____ theory.

(A) functionalist   (D) enthnomethodologist

(B) conflict   (E) dramaturgical

(C) interactionist

72. According to the concept of the "looking-glass self," we come to understand ourselves by

(A) resolving the issue of trust versus mistrust.

(B) bringing closure to our Oedipus complex.

(C) imagining how others view us.

(D) resolving our early parent-child conflicts.

(E) dealing with our innate feelings of inferiority.

73. In the socialization process in the United States, which group or individual comes to take on special importance during adolescence?

(A) Parents, regardless of one's gender

(B) Peer groups

(C) Fathers, especially for male adolescents

(D) Professional educators, such as teachers and counselors

(E) Mothers, regardless of one's gender

74. Students in a classroom and workers in an office are examples of what type of group?

(A) Primary

(B) Secondary

(C) Expressive

(D) Mob

(E) Social movement

75. A number of people are waiting for a bus. They do not interact with each other, and they have no sense of belonging together. This is called a(n)

(A) aggregate.

(B) secondary group.

(C) primary group.

(D) mob.

(E) group.

76. Sociologists refer to any violation of the law as

(A) a felony.

(B) a deviant act.

(C) juvenile delinquency.

(D) white-collar crime.

(E) crime.

77. The biological potential to give birth is called

(A) eugenics.

(B) genetics.

(C) fertility.

(D) fecundity.

(E) population growth.

78. "Push" factors in migration include all of the following EXCEPT

(A) religious intolerance.

(B) unemployment.

(C) travel costs.

(D) poor climatic conditions.

(E) political oppression.

79. Cities differ from rural areas in all of the following ways EXCEPT that cities

    (A) have lower birth rates.

    (B) are centers of industry.

    (C) have fewer moral values.

    (D) are centers of commerce and trade.

    (E) have a greater concentration of people.

80. According to Emile Durkheim, people in small, traditional communities are held together by

    (A) mechanical solidarity.

    (B) organic solidarity.

    (C) formal legal codes.

    (D) practices that allow for diversity.

    (E) None of the above.

81. Since 1970, the largest growth in the United States has been in which of the following areas?

    (A) Northeastern urban centers

    (B) Southern cities

    (C) Rural areas

    (D) The suburbs

    (E) The exurbs

82. The development of new strains of wheat and rice that substantially increase the crop yield is called

    (A) the agricultural revolution. (D) agribusiness.

    (B) the green revolution.   (E) collectivism.

    (C) scientific farming.

83. The study of patterns of change in cities that result from the processes of competition, natural selection, and evolution is called

(A) conflict theory.   (D) urbanization.

(B) social Darwinism.   (E) modernization.

(C) urban ecology.

84. An organized effort to promote some form of social change is called

(A) collective behavior.   (D) a social movement.

(B) mob behavior.   (E) a crowd.

(C) a riot.

85. The formalized enactment of religious beliefs is called

(A) dogma.   (D) revelations.

(B) rituals.   (E) ecumenical events.

(C) churches.

86. Command that is recognized and accepted, and in which a person is given the right to make decisions is called

(A) power.   (D) influence.

(B) coercion.   (E) law.

(C) authority.

87. *Brown v. Board of Education* (1954) was a Supreme Court case that declared what activity to be unconstitutional?

(A) Gender discrimination

(B) Discrimination in hiring

(C) Laws against interracial marriages

(D) School segregation

(E) Discrimination in housing

88. A company that has holdings in a number of different industries is called a

(A) multinational.   (D) conglomerate.

(B) corporation.   (E) monopoly.

(C) legal partnership.

89. Teachers, secretaries, and accountants are considered

    (A) blue-collar workers.

    (B) white-collar workers.

    (C) workers with high prestige.

    (D) workers with low prestige.

    (E) members of the working class.

90. With the decline in manufacturing and the rise in service industries, along with the growing importance of computers, automation, and communication technology, many sociologists now argue we are living in a(n) _____ society.

    (A) recreational   (D) postindustrial

    (B) capitalist   (E) industrial

    (C) competitive

91. Which of the following factors does not increase the likelihood of divorce?

    (A) Low socioeconomic status

    (B) High socioeconomic status

    (C) Early age at marriage

    (D) Urban locale

    (E) Short dating period

92. Inequality and discrimination that result from the regular workings of a society is called

    (A) prejudice   (D) annihilation.

    (B) racism.   (E) subjugation.

    (C) institutionalized racism.

93. Sarah's mother was a cashier at a local supermarket, and Sarah is a professor of biology at a university. This is an example of

    (A) intragenerational mobility.

(B) structural mobility.

(C) intergenerational mobility.

(D) horizontal mobility.

(E) immigrant mobility.

94. The majority of poor people in the United States are

(A) lazy.

(B) black.

(C) white.

(D) single men.

(E) Latino.

95. The idea that all Irish Americans are alcoholics, or all African Americans are lazy is an example of

(A) prejudice.

(B) discrimination.

(C) stereotypes.

(D) the authoritarian personality.

(E) scapegoating.

96. An increase in the number of people living in the cities along with an increased influence of these cities is called

(A) gentrification.

(B) suburbanization.

(C) rural renaissance.

(D) urbanization.

(E) incumbent upgrading.

97. The term the "second shift" refers to the fact that a number of women

(A) are still responsible for housework in addition to working outside the home.

(B) work more than one job.

(C) work off hours, earlier or later than 9:00 A.M. to 5:00 P.M.

(D) contribute relatively little to the family income.

(E) have earnings equal to men for comparable work.

98. Patterns of social life that appear in all societies are called

    (A) norms.   (D) laws.

    (B) folkways.   (E) fashions.

    (C) cultural universals.

99. Max Weber created models of social phenomenon which he believed contained the essential elements of the phenomenon under study. He called these models

    (A) theories.   (D) ideal types.

    (B) constructs.   (E) variables.

    (C) concepts.

100. Louis is a carpenter. Because of automation, machinery will now do the manual work he used to do. His company sends him for retraining. Upon his return he will receive a promotion to computer specialist. Louis is experiencing

    (A) immigrant mobility.   (D) individual mobility.

    (B) structural mobility.   (E) horizontal mobility.

    (C) downward mobility.

CLEP INTRODUCTORY SOCIOLOGY
TEST 2

ANSWER KEY

1.	(B)	26.	(C)	51.	(C)	76.	(E)
2.	(A)	27.	(E)	52.	(B)	77.	(D)
3.	(D)	28.	(D)	53.	(D)	78.	(C)
4.	(B)	29.	(A)	54.	(A)	79.	(C)
5.	(A)	30.	(C)	55.	(A)	80.	(A)
6.	(D)	31.	(B)	56.	(C)	81.	(D)
7.	(E)	32.	(A)	57.	(E)	82.	(B)
8.	(D)	33.	(D)	58.	(A)	83.	(C)
9.	(A)	34.	(E)	59.	(E)	84.	(D)
10.	(B)	35.	(C)	60.	(C)	85.	(B)
11.	(B)	36.	(B)	61.	(D)	86.	(C)
12.	(E)	37.	(C)	62.	(E)	87.	(D)
13.	(B)	38.	(B)	63.	(D)	88.	(D)
14.	(D)	39.	(B)	64.	(E)	89.	(B)
15.	(B)	40.	(A)	65.	(E)	90.	(D)
16.	(C)	41.	(C)	66.	(C)	91.	(B)
17.	(E)	42.	(E)	67.	(B)	92.	(C)
18.	(D)	43.	(C)	68.	(B)	93.	(C)
19.	(C)	44.	(D)	69.	(C)	94.	(C)
20.	(A)	45.	(D)	70.	(D)	95.	(C)
21.	(D)	46.	(B)	71.	(E)	96.	(D)
22.	(B)	47.	(B)	72.	(C)	97.	(A)
23.	(E)	48.	(D)	73.	(B)	98.	(C)
24.	(B)	49.	(D)	74.	(B)	99.	(D)
25.	(C)	50.	(E)	75.	(A)	100.	(B)

DETAILED EXPLANATIONS OF ANSWERS

TEST 2

1. **(B)** Emile Durkheim is the author of one of the first classic sociological studies, *Suicide*. He, Weber, and Marx are considered to be the three major "founding fathers" of sociology. The contribution of the other four sociologists were not to the study of suicide. (A) Weber's contributions include studies on world religions and bureaucracy. (C) Marx is best known for his study of the development of capitalism. (D) Talcott Parsons, a major figure in American sociology, developed the theoretical school known as Structural Functionalist. (E) Auguste Comte is best known for coining the term "sociology."

2. **(A)** The mean is one of three statistical measures known as measures of central tendency. The mean is calculated by adding all of the test scores and dividing by the number of tests. In this case, the total of all test scores is 420. This number divided by the five tests equals 84. The two other measures of central tendency are the median and the mode. The median is the midpoint score—50 percent of all scores are above it, and 50 percent of all scores are below it. In this example, the median is 83. The mode is the score that appears most often. In this example there is no modal category because each score appears only once.

3. **(D)** The theory of the demographic transition describes the process by which societies move from high birth and death rates to low birth and death rates as a consequence of industrialization. The final stage of the process is indicated by choice (D). (B) High birth rates and low death rates occur during the transitional phase of the demographic transition. (C) Low birth rates and high death rates is not a phase in the theory. (E) While changes in agricultural output may play a role in causing the transition, it is not considered part of the theory itself.

4.   **(B)**   Amalgamation is the best answer because it involves the physical absorption of one group by another group through intermarriage. (A) Separation may be viewed as the opposite of amalgamation. It is the desire to maintain a separate identity from other groups in society. (C) Cultural pluralism holds that different groups may be allowed to maintain certain "old-world traditions" while still assimilating to the new culture. (D) Segregation involves the physical separation of peoples. (E) Multiculturalism pertains to the awareness of racial and ethnic differences that exist within a society.

5.   **(A)**   According to classic Marxist theory there are two groups who are in perpetual conflict in capitalist societies: the bourgeoisie and the proletariat. The bourgeoisie is the term Marx used for the class that owns the means of production. (B) The proletariat are the workers of society. (C) Intellectual elites do not own the means of production, and they do not play a role in this theory. (D) White, Anglo-Saxon Protestants are often viewed as the dominant group in American society, but Marx did not mention them in his theory. (E) The Fortune 500 are the wealthiest corporations in America as listed by *Fortune* magazine; they have nothing to do with Marxist theory.

6.   **(D)**   Societies have different norms with respect to marriages. Some societies have a norm of polygyny, which allows men to have more than one wife at the same time. (A) Monogamy is when one may have only one mate at a time. (B) Serial monogamy is when one may have a number of mates, but only one at a time. (C) Polygamy is the general term used to refer to having more than one mate at a time regardless of gender, but it doesn't specifically identify more than one wife, as the question specifies. (E) Polyandry is the rarest marital norm. This is when a woman is permitted to have more than one husband at the same time.

7.   **(E)**   Sigmund Freud created the terms id, ego, and superego to describe the key components of the personality. Much of the work in the field of child development is in response to Freud's original writings. (A) Piaget is best known for his work on children's intellectual development. (B) Kohlberg's name is associated with the issue of moral development. Mead (C) and Cooley (D) were both American sociologists who worked in the field of socialization and human social development.

8.   **(D)**   Oligopoly is when several corporations, usually four or less, control an industry. (A) A monopoly is when one corporation controls an

industry. (B) Conglomerates are large corporations that have interest in a variety of industries. (C) Economic elite is a term developed by C. Wright Mills to describe the concentration of power in society. (E) Societies that have economies based on a variety of industrial endeavors are involved in economic diversification.

9. **(A)** Howard is experiencing a classic example of role conflict. His responsibilities as a student and as a worker are in conflict in the hypothetical situation presented. (B) Role strain is the difficulty in fulfilling the obligations of a particular role which can occur because of role conflict or many other circumstances. Trauma (C), cognitive dissonance (D), and emotional distress (E) are all psychological terms related to emotional reactions to stressful situations.

10. **(B)** Reform movements seek to make some changes in society but not radical or revolutionary changes in society's structure. (A) Expressive movements tend to focus on emotional or personal issues rather than societal change. (C) Revolutionary movements often call for dramatic and substantive changes in a society. (D) Mob behavior, by definition, is not a social movement. It involves random, disorganized, and temporary actions of relatively small numbers of people. (E) Radical movements often offer extreme alternatives to the way a society is currently functioning.

11. **(B)** Jose and Maria come from the same ethnic and religious groups, and therefore are following the norm of endogamy, which states that one should marry within one's own social group. (A) Exogamy is the norm which forces persons to marry outside of a particular group, as illustrated by the incest taboo. (C) Arranged marriages are arranged by persons other than the bride and groom. There is no indication of this occurring in the example. (D) The stimulus-value-role theory describes how specific individuals are selected as dating partners. (E) Polyandrous marriages are when women are permitted to be married to more than one man at the same time.

12. **(E)** Karl Marx, the father of conflict theory, argued that religion serves as an "opiate" for the poor, leading them to accept their subordinate status in society. (A) Weber was one of the leading figures in the study of comparative religion. (B) Tonnies' work concentrated on the study of community. (C) Freud is the father of psychoanalysis. (D) Durkheim saw religion as having important social functions; most importantly, as an element that helps to hold societies together.

13. **(B)**   Monotheism is the belief in one god. Islam teaches the existence of one supreme god, Allah. (A) Animism is the belief that spirits inhabit both animate and inanimate objects. (C) Polytheism is the belief in many gods. (D) Theism is the belief that gods directly interfere in human activities. (E) An atheist does not believe in the existence of god or gods.

14. **(D)**   Tracking involves placing students in classes based upon certain predetermined categories. (A) Testing out is a method of skipping classes based on one's ability to pass certain examinations. (B) Latent functions of education are the unintended consequences of the educational institution. (C) Manifest functions of education are the intended and overt consequences of the educational institution. (E) Biased placement often results when the tracking system is imposed on a school system.

15. **(B)**   Traditional authority assumes that the norms of the past are still legitimate in the present. (A) Legal-rational authority asserts that persons in positions of authority have clearly defined obligations and responsibilities that are to be impersonally administered. (C) Charismatic authority tends to be revolutionary and is based upon the unique characteristics of the person. (D) Court precedent is when court decisions build upon one another to create a body of law. (E) A system of sanctions is the manner in which societies enforce the norms of the culture.

16. **(C)**   Most societies have a combination of free enterprise and government-controlled economic systems. (A) Capitalist economic systems allow for free enterprise, competition, and the drive for profit. (B) Socialist economies involve centralized control of the economic system. (D) Laissez-faire is the French term often associated with the concept of the free enterprise system. (E) Communist economies call for the total control of a society's economic system.

17. **(E)**   Totalitarian states traditionally have only one political party, the party in power. Totalitarian governments attempt to control all of the social institutions of society. The government then attempts to legitimate this control by creating an ideological system that supports the government's position.

18. **(D)**   Lobbying is the attempt to influence the government's decision-making process. (A) Bribery is the illegal act of trying to buy off a public official. (B) There is nothing illegal in trying to influence government policies. (C) White-collar crime refers to illegal acts committed by persons in

legitimate positions. Lobbying is not illegal. (E) Deviant behavior assumes behavior is unacceptable by the ethical or legal standards of society.

19. **(C)** While media are very important to society, they are not viewed as one of the major social institutions. Social institutions focus on fulfilling basic social and biological needs such as procreation. Family (A), economy (B), government (D), and education (E), along with religion, are the five basic social institutions.

20. **(A)** The functionalist theory sees society as made up of interdependent parts that work to maintain a stable state for society. (B) Conflict theory focuses on the potential for conflict and social change. (C) Symbolic interactionist theory examines how individuals and groups come to define the society around them. (D) Ethnomethodology looks at the everyday events which make up the social world. (E) Dramaturgy borrows language from the theater to examine how we play roles in everyday social interactions.

21. **(D)** A variable is a characteristic that varies from individual to individual or group to group. An example of a variable would be educational attainment. (A) A concept is a mental image or generalized idea. (B) A symbol is one thing that is taken to represent another thing. (C) A hypothesis is a testable proposition. (E) An experiment is a type of methodology where the experimenter controls the variable being studied.

22. **(B)** A longitudinal study follows a group of individuals over a substantial period of time. (A) Cross-sectional studies usually occur at one period in time, and look at a cross-section of the population. (C) Open-ended interviews are usually one time in-depth interviews with one subject at a time. (D) Participant observation studies involve the researcher participating in the group (s)he is studying. (E) Surveys are usually given out at one point in time to ask questions of a large group of people on any variety of topics.

23. **(E)** Ethnocentrism is looking at other societies through the beliefs of one's own culture. (A) Prejudice is developing preconceived notions about other persons because of the group they belong to. (B) Discrimination is the unfair treatment of people because of their racial, religious, or ethnic background. (C) Bias is to show preference for someone or some group. (D) Culture shock is sometimes the reaction that occurs when an individual enters a new and different cultural setting.

24. **(B)** All three groups may be classified as subcultures. These are groups that exist in society but have some distinctive characteristics which set them apart from their fellow citizens. (A) Countercultures are subcultures whose values and beliefs challenge those of mainstream society; this would not necessarily characterize these groups. (C) Jewish Americans constitute an ethnic group but police officers and college students do not. (D) None of the groups listed can be considered a racial group. (E) Social classes are determined by socioeconomic characteristics, and none of these groups would necessarily constitute a social class.

25. **(C)** The idea that we give meaning to the world around us is central to the interactionist approach. (A) Functionalist theory focuses on the functions of social institutions in society. (B) Conflict theorists examine the economic inequalities that exist in society. (D) Social exchange theory argues that rational decision making dictates the nature of social interactions. (E) Dramaturgy examines how we create images of ourselves that we attempt to communicate to others.

26. **(C)** In primary groups members tend to have varied and substantial knowledge of other members. Primary groups are typically small in number (A), last for very long periods of time (B), and intimate communication (D) is the norm.

27. **(E)** All of the answers are elements of a bureaucracy as noted by Weber. Other characteristics noted by Weber include a clear-cut division of responsibilities in the different positions in the bureaucracy, promotion based upon merit, and a clear-cut separation between one's position in a bureaucracy and their private life.

28. **(D)** Anomie, a term developed by Emile Durkheim, is defined as being in a state of normlessness. (A) Alienation is related to anomie. It refers to a sense of not belonging to society. (B) Fatalism is a belief that one has no control over one's own life. (C) Cognitive dissonance is when one continues to believe in something in the face of contrary evidence. (E) Innovation is utilizing novel approaches to old problems.

29. **(A)** Labeling theory describes how individuals come to be defined as deviant. Primary and secondary deviance are elements in this theory. (B) Differential association analyzes how one comes to learn deviant norms and values. (C) Control theory focuses on the concept of conformity. (D) Techniques of neutralization describes how persons may ratio-

nalize their involvement in deviant behavior. (E) Strain theory discusses how individuals may utilize illegitimate means to achieve legitimate goals.

30. **(C)** Most sociologists assert that gender differences are largely a result of our upbringing or socialization. (A) While biology dictates our sex, what it means to be male or female is a sociological phenomenon. (B) Sociologists focus on large groups and tend not to examine individual psychological characteristics. (D) The Oedipus complex, developed by Freud, is a theory concerning the psycho-sexual development of boys. (E) Sociobiology holds the view that much of our social behavior is genetically determined. Most sociologists take a dim view of this theory.

31. **(B)** Malthus is one of the most influential figures in the history of the study of population. Urban problems (A), economic problems (C), politics (D), and education (E) are all related to population issues; however, Malthus is most closely associated with the study of population.

32. **(A)** *Gemeinschaft* is the term Tonnies used to describe the small, intimate communities of the past. (B) *Gesellschaft* is the term Tonnies used to describe modern, urban society. (C) Urban refers to cities which are often seen as impersonal. (D) Modern and urban are usually related in the sense that the modern displaces the traditional, and personal relationships are replaced by impersonal ones. (E) An industrialized society has moved toward a modern, urban condition where industrialization has replaced agriculture as a focus of economic activity.

33. **(D)** Assimilation is a theory that focuses on the absorption of new groups into a society. (A) Concentric zone theory argues that cities develop in a series of concentric zones from the center out. (B) Sector theory states that cities emerge along major transportation routes. (C) Multiple-nuclei theory asserts that any one city might have a number of different centers.

34. **(E)** Diffusion is the migration of ideas, beliefs, and technology from one culture to another. (A) Invasion assumes a forced encroachment of one group onto the territory of another. (B) Acculturation is the process by which immigrants absorb the culture of their new society. (C) Evolution is the slow process of adaptation that occurs in nature. (D) Culture conflict is the first experience of two cultures coming into contact. It may lead to diffusion, but it does not refer to the diffusion of things itself.

35. **(C)** The statement in the question is a classic definition of evolutionary theory as it applies to societies. (A) Functionalist theory focuses on what holds societies together. (B) Conflict theory emphasizes the importance of conflict in societal change. (D) Interactionist theory examines the micro-level of social life. (E) Revolution is the concept which defines dramatic changes or radical changes in society.

36. **(B)** Conflict theory emphasizes the competition over societal resources including the resource of power. (A) Functionalist theory emphasizes continuity and the relatedness of social institutions, rather than change. (C) Interactionist theory examines the everyday encounters of members of society, and how we come to derive meaning out of our social interaction. (D) Evolutionary theory sees societies as changing in a gradual manner, evolving from simpler to more complex societies.

37. **(C)** C. Wright Mills' concept of the sociological imaginations links individual biography to what occurs in the larger social and cultural setting. (A) Mills' concept is sociological and does not include psychological predispositions. (B) While family background is important in one's life, it is not central to Mills' ideas. (D) Racial identity, too, is important but not specific to this concept. (E) Population patterns do impact society but are not discussed by Mills.

38. **(B)** The "Chicago School" was and is a well-known center for the study of urban development. (A) Harvard was a center for the development of functionalism. (C) North Carolina has a fine reputation for empirical studies. (D) The University of Pennsylvania is well-known for its population studies. (E) New York University is known for the study of criminology.

39. **(B)** George Herbert Mead described socialization as a process of movement from the play stage to the game stage during which a generalized other emerged. The other four theorists did not use these concepts. (A) Sigmund Freud was the father of psychoanalysis. (C) Charles Horton Cooley developed the concept of the looking-glass self. (D) Erik Erikson analyzed human development in eight distinct stages. (E) Levinson examined adult socialization.

40. **(A)** Stratification is the general term used to describe how societies place its members into specific categories. (B) Social mobility refers to movement from one social position to another. (C) Status inconsistency is

when a person ranks differently on different social characteristics. (D) The power elite is C. Wright Mills' theory about the distribution of power in society. (E) Social evaluation is the process by which we place individuals in social categories.

41. **(C)**   Because both positions have approximately the same status, we can say Martin has moved horizontally. (A) Upward mobility denotes an increase in one's status position. (B) Downward mobility involves a decrease in status. (D) Status inconsistency involves a conflict in status positions. (E) In order to know if Martin experienced intergenerational mobility, we would have to know the status of Martin's father, which is not stated in the problem.

42. **(E)**   Intragenerational mobility is a change in social status within one's lifetime. (A) Intergenerational change is change that occurs between generations. (B) Intragenerational change may lead to status inconsistency, but this does not always occur. (C) This type of change may also result in downward mobility. (D) Family wealth determines one's position at birth, but it does not determine intragenerational change.

43. **(C)**   Cultural relativism asserts that cultures should be studied without imposing the values and beliefs of the observer's culture. (A) Ethnocentrism is the opposite of cultural relativism. It imposes the values of the observer's culture upon the culture under study. (B) Cultural pluralism implies that immigrant groups may still maintain some "old-world traditions" while they assimilate into a new society. (D) Anthropology and (E) sociology are social science disciplines that study cultures and societies and adopt a posture of cultural relativism, but they are not the belief itself.

44. **(D)**   Karl Marx is seen as the father of conflict theory. (A) Freud is the founding father of the psychoanalytic movement. (B) Parsons helped develop functionalism in the United States. (C) Merton expanded functionalist thought in the United States. (E) Mead is one of the key figures in symbolic interactionism.

45. **(D)**   The French writer Comte first used the term "sociology" in the nineteenth century. (A) Marx is the father of conflict theory. (B) Weber wrote on a number of topics central to the discipline of sociology. (C) Durkheim wrote the first sociological study of suicide. (E) Tonnies analyzed the different types of communities.

46. **(B)**   Genocide and annihilation refer to the physical destruction of a people. (A) Expulsion is the forced emigration of a group. (C) Assimilation is the absorption of an immigrant group into a new society. (D) Amalgamation is the biological fusion of two or more groups. (E) Segregation is the separation of two or more groups.

47. **(B)**   Ascribed status is status determined at birth. It is usually associated with rigid systems of stratification such as castes. (A) Achieved status is a characteristic of a mobile society. Both intergenerational (C) and intragenerational (D) mobility occur fairly rarely in a caste-like society. Since ascribed status is a characteristic of a caste system, (E) is wrong.

48. **(D)**   C. Wright Mills did not include the media elite in his formulation of the power elite. Military (A), economic (B), and political (C) are the three components of the power elite. Since the media elite are not included in his concept, (E) is wrong.

49. **(D)**   Prestige is the concept sociologists use to refer to such respect and approval. The other four choices are wrong because they refer to different sociological processes. (A) Power is the ability to control others. (B) Influence is often viewed as indirect power. (C) Social class is one's social position in society. Social class can be based partly on prestige, but is a much broader concept. (E) Authority is legitimate and recognized power.

50. **(E)**   Bellhops have lower prestige than the other occupations listed. Compared to the other occupations, bellhops require less education and training. The other occupations are listed in order of their prestige rankings.

51. **(C)**   Women have experienced the largest increase in labor force participation. (A) Teenagers traditionally have relatively low levels of labor force activity. (B) Men's participation has been somewhat consistent over time. Both blacks (D) and Latinos (E) tend to have high rates of unemployment. This is due to lower levels of educational attainment and historical discrimination in the labor market.

52. **(B)** The median is the midpoint number. (A) The mean is the statistical average. (C) The mode is the number that appears most often. (D) Average is the same as the mean.

53. **(D)** Sociology emerged in the nineteenth century with the work of people such as Auguste Comte, Karl Marx, and Emile Durkheim. (A) The sixteenth century was the period of the Renaissance. (B) The seventeenth century saw the expansion of European influence in the New World. (C) Some of the ideas that emerged in the eighteenth century contributed to the development of sociology. (E) The influence of sociology increased substantially during the twentieth century.

54. **(A)** Intelligence does not determine social class position. Intelligence is an individual characteristic that is distributed throughout the stratification system. Economic position (B), social status (C), and political power (D) are the three elements in Weber's analysis of stratification.

55. **(A)** The upper class is characterized by "old money," or wealth that is inherited. (B) The upper-middle class often includes people who make great fortunes on their own. (C) The lower-middle class makes up much of what is called the white-collar population and does not inherit much wealth. (D) The working class is made up of blue-collar workers and does not possess wealth. (E) The lower class is the poorest segment of society.

56. **(C)** Class systems are more open to the possibility of social mobility as compared to the other choices. (A) Caste systems tend to be the most closed of all social systems with little social mobility. (B) Estate systems also tend to be closed, but not quite to the extent of caste systems. (D) Ascribed status implies that one's position is determined at birth. (E) Tradition-based systems tend to limit the possibility for social mobility.

57. **(E)** All facets of one's life are influenced, at least in part, by one's social class. (A) There is a direct relationship between social class and educational attainment. (B) Research has indicated that different social classes utilize different strategies in raising their children. (C) Opportunities in the labor force are largely determined by social class. (D) Recreational activities also appear to follow certain social class patterns.

58. **(A)** Patriarchy is the belief that power should reside in the male population. (B) Matriarchy is the belief that power should be in the control

of the female population. (C) Patrilineal is emphasizing the male line of descent. (D) Patrilocal refers to the norm that newlyweds will reside with the groom's family. (E) The term paternal refers to the male line of ascent.

59. **(E)**   The unequal distribution of power by gender is the focus of conflict theory. (A) Intelligence is not gender related. (B) Physical strength, by itself, does not appear to play a role in patriarchal systems. (C) There is no evidence concerning the subconscious fears of men. (D) There is no evidence that men envy the woman's ability to bear children.

60. **(C)**   Women earn approximately 70 percent of what men earn. Research indicates that this holds true even when education and training are held constant. Even at the highest levels of education, female college graduates still earn only 70 percent of what male college graduates earn. The figure of 70 percent has been somewhat consistent over the past ten years. Therefore, the other choices are incorrect.

61. **(D)**   Minority groups both share certain characteristics and are victimized by discriminatory behavior. (A) An ethnic group shares cultural traditions. (B) A racial group is perceived to share similar physical characteristics. (C) A majority group is not likely to be victims of discrimination. (E) A marginal group may or may not be victims of discrimination. More information would be necessary to make that determination.

62. **(E)**   In Merton's analysis all four are part of his typology. (A) The first type includes persons who do not feel prejudice and do not participate in discriminatory behavior. (B) The second type does not feel prejudice, but due to social pressure may participate in discrimination. (C) The third type has prejudicial feelings but does not discriminate. (D) The fourth type has no opportunity to act out his or her prejudicial feelings.

63. **(D)**   Cultural pluralism is the pattern whereby ethnic groups still maintain some linkages to their "old-world" culture. (A) Assimilation is the general term used to describe a variety of immigrant patterns, and the process by which new groups become absorbed into society. (B) Anglo-conformity assumes immigrants will give up all of their "old-world" customs. (C) The melting pot refers to high rates of intermarriage among different ethnic and racial groups. (E) Subjugation is when one group is completely dominated by another group.

64. **(E)**   All of the choices are considered functions of the family. (A) Families regulate sexual behavior through the incest taboo. (B) Many consider the socializing of children the most important family function. (C) The family one is born into determines one's initial social position in society. (D) Affections and companionship are considered newer functions of the family.

65. **(E)**   The average number of children per family has decreased over the past 30 years. (A) Many studies indicate that premarital sexual behavior has increased. (B) The number of working wives/mothers has increased substantially in the recent past. (C) Household size has declined steadily since the mid-1960s. (D) Single parenthood is a major trend in family life today.

66. **(C)**   Millenarian movements see the destruction of the world as imminent. (A) These movements have occurred through the world. (B) Spirituality is present in almost all religious movements, and it is difficult to objectively assess differences in levels of spirituality. (D) These movements have also occurred in modern societies. (E) Millenarian movements would be similar to radical or revolutionary social movements.

67. **(B)**   Secularization is the process of becoming less influenced by religious beliefs. (A) This is the opposite of secularization. (C) Religious revelation would lose influence in a secular society. (D) Secular societies tend to look ahead as opposed to looking back. (E) Religious interpretation, new or old, would tend to lose influence in a secular society.

68. **(B)**   Functionalists would generally not view educational institutions as sources for social change. (A) A manifest function of education is to teach children basic academic skills. (C) The school experience is part of a child's socialization process. (D) All school systems have as a function the preparation of young people for citizenship.

69. **(C)**   Demography is the scientific study of population. (A) Anthropologists study both preliterate and modern cultures. (B) Sociology is the scientific study of social behavior. (D) Fecundity is the biological potential to give birth. (E) Geography focuses on the physical characteristics of the earth.

70. **(D)**   Sexism is an ideology that offers justification for a belief in male dominance. (A) Prejudice is the general term used to describe the

pre-judgment of others and is not limited to gender. (B) Racism is the ideology that legitimates the belief in racial superiority. (C) Discrimination refers to unequal treatment of persons because of the group they belong to. (E) Ethnocentrism is judging others based upon the values and beliefs of your own group.

71. **(E)** Dramaturgy views people as actors and utilizes the language of the theater. (A) Functionalist theory examines how social institutions perform specific functions for society. (B) Conflict theory focuses on the competition for societal resources. (C) Interactionist theory analyzes how people create meaning out of their everyday experiences. (D) Ethnomethodology looks at typical everyday social encounters.

72. **(C)** The looking-glass self involves our imagination and how we believe others feel about us. (A) Trust versus mistrust comes from the psycho-social theory of Erik Erikson. (B) The Oedipus complex is a concept developed by Sigmund Freud in his psychoanalytic theory. (D) Early parent-child conflict is an issue addressed by a number of developmental theories but not by the looking-glass approach. (E) Questions of inferiority derive from the work of the psychoanalyst Alfred Adler and are not addressed by the looking-glass approach.

73. **(B)** In American culture, peers become very significant during the adolescent period. (A) One's parents tend to have less influence during adolescence. (C) Males begin to look for other role models during this period of development. (D) Professional educators, while important, do not play as major a role as do peers during adolescence. (E) Although mothers play an important role, many times they must compete with peers with respect to influencing their adolescent children.

74. **(B)** Secondary groups are impersonal, and their members do not have emotional links. (A) A primary group involves emotional linkages. (C) Expressive groups involve the emotional connections between their members. (D) A mob is a temporary aggregate with no long-term commitment. (E) A social movement involves a large number of people who seek some change in society.

75. **(A)** An aggregate is a group of people who are in the same physical place at the same time but have no connection to one another. (B) A secondary group would have some purpose for interaction, such as fellow workers in a factory. (C) A primary group is a personal intimate group.

(D) A mob acts in a random fashion directed toward a short-term goal. (E) A group consists of people who interact in face-to-face encounters over a period of time.

76. **(E)** Sociologists refer to any violation of law as a crime, regardless of the seriousness of the behavior. (A) A felony is the most serious criminal behavior, such as homicide. (B) A deviant act may or may not be a crime, depending upon the criminal code. (C) Juvenile delinquency is a category of crime that depends upon the age of the perpetrator. (D) White-collar crime is crime committed by person in respectable positions.

77. **(D)** Fecundity is the demographic term used to describe the biological potential to have children. (A) Eugenics is the notion that we can improve human genetic stock. (B) Genetics is the study of genes. (C) Fertility is the actual number of births a woman will have. (E) Population growth is a result of fertility and mortality.

78. **(C)** Travel costs constitute intervening variables that must be considered in the decision to migrate. Push factors are those factors that force one out of an area. Pull factors are factors that attract one to an area. Religious intolerance (A), unemployment (B), poor climatic conditions (D), and political oppression (E) are all classic push factors. Historically, the major push factor has been unemployment or the inability to support oneself and one's family.

79. **(C)** Cities have different values than do rural areas. Whether or not these values are better or worse than those that exist in rural areas is not a sociological question. The response would depend upon the values of the observer. (A) Cities do have lower birth rates than do rural areas. Cities are centers of industry (B), commerce, and trade (D). (E) Cities, by definition, have a greater concentration of people.

80. **(A)** For Durkheim, mechanical solidarity is the social glue that keeps members of rural societies together. (B) Organic solidarity is the term Durkheim used to describe the attempt at consensus in urban areas. (C) Formal legal codes tend to appear with the development of cities. (D) Diversity is usually unacceptable in rural societies.

81. **(D)** Major growth in the United States has occurred in the suburbs. Almost half the populations now live in suburban areas. (A) Northeastern urban areas have experienced a decline in population. (B) Southern cities

have experienced growth but not to the same degree as the suburbs. (C) Rural areas have been in a state of population decline. (E) The exurbs are older rural areas that are being converted into suburbs.

82. **(B)** The Green Revolution refers to the development of what are sometimes referred to as "super crops." They yield more food per acre than do traditionally grown strains. (A) The agricultural revolution occurred approximately 10,000 to 15,000 years ago with the invention of farming. (C) Scientific farming is the use of modern scientific techniques in agriculture. It led to the Green Revolution. (D) Agribusiness is the development of very large farm corporations. (E) Collectivism was the technique used in the former Soviet Union to stimulate their agricultural output. It did not succeed.

83. **(C)** Urban ecologists study urban development and change utilizing the model of an ecosystem. (A) Conflict theory is sometimes used in urban ecology but is not synonymous with it. (B) Social Darwinism utilized evolutionary theory to study societies as a whole. (D) Urbanization is the process that is studied by urban ecologists. (E) Modernization is a general term used to describe evolutionary change in all of society.

84. **(D)** A social movement is a somewhat organized attempt to change some element in society or society itself. (A) A social movement is one form of collective behavior, which is a more general concept. (B) Mob behavior is short-lived with no determinate goals. (C) A riot is a short-lived and often violent reaction to a real or imagined event. (E) A crowd is a group of people who share a common space.

85. **(B)** Rituals are actions which have religious significance for the participants. (A) Dogma is a system of doctrine of a religion. (C) Churches are the organizations and structures central to religions. (D) Revelation is seen as a result of participating in rituals. (E) Ecumenical events occur when representatives of more than one religion join together in ceremonies.

86. **(C)** Authority is legitimate power. (A) Power may be recognized and accepted or not. It is the ability to control others. (B) Coercion is forcing one to accept your decisions. (D) Influence is the ability to sway others' views. It may derive from legitimate power or not. (E) Laws are norms that are codified and supported by the state and are a result of legitimate power.

87. **(D)** This landmark case declared that the idea of "separate but equal" schooling was unconstitutional. (A) Discrimination based on gender was made illegal by the Civil Rights Act of 1964. (B) Discrimination in hiring is against the law because of a series of federal and local laws. (C) Bans against interracial marriages were declared unconstitutional in 1967 *(Loving v. Virginia)*. (E) Discrimination in housing is against the law because of a number of federal and local laws.

88. **(D)** A conglomerate is one company that has control of other companies in a variety of economic activities. (A) A multinational is a company that does business in a number of countries. (B) A corporation is a company that is publicly owned, and where investors have limited liability. A corporation may or may not have holdings in different industries. (C) A legal partnership is similar to a corporation but where there are a limited number of owners. (E) A monopoly is when one company controls an industry.

89. **(B)** All three occupations would be classified as white-collar. (A) Blue-collar workers usually wear uniforms to work, and usually engage in manual labor. (C) While teachers and accountants may have high prestige, generally, secretaries do not. (D) Accountants and teachers are seen as having high prestige. (E) The working class is a term used by sociologists to denote members of a particular social class that is below the middle class. Teachers and accountants are part of the middle class, and in some cases secretaries may also be viewed as part of the middle class.

90. **(D)** Many jobs have been lost to technology while new jobs have developed which involve intellectual work. This has been termed the postindustrial society. (A) As a result of this development, it is thought that there will be more time for recreational activities. This does not seem to have occurred yet. (B) Capitalism is one form of economic activity. Most societies have mixed economies. (C) Competition is part of both industrial and postindustrial societies. (E) Industrial societies were dominant in the nineteenth century, and for a good part of the twentieth century, but are being replaced by the postindustrial society.

91. **(B)** There is an inverse relationship between socioeconomic status and divorce. The higher one's status, the lower the divorce rate. (A) Low economic position increases the chance for divorce. (C) Young age at marriage is a strong predictor of divorce, especially if one of the parties is in her (his) teens. (D) Divorce rates are higher in urban areas. (E) A short dating period is also associated with high divorce rates.

92. **(C)**   Institutionalized racism results from the usual customs and traditions of the society. (A) Prejudice is the prejudgment of others because of the group they belong to. (B) Racism is the ideology that legitimates prejudice and discrimination. (D) Annihilation is the physical destruction of a people. (E) Subjugation is the conscious attempt to subordinate a group.

93. **(C)**   This is intergenerational mobility because Sarah has achieved a higher status than her mother. (A) Intragenerational mobility is mobility within one generation. (B) Structural mobility is due to changes in the economic system, but nothing is mentioned about this in the problem. (D) Horizontal mobility is moving from one status to a similar status. (E) Immigrant mobility is due to the movement of older immigrant groups because of the entrance of new immigrant groups.

94. **(C)**   In total numbers, most poor are white. (B) is wrong because, while there are proportionately more blacks who are poor, blacks are not a numerical majority of the poor. (A) Most people classified as poor work; therefore, the idea that poor people are lazy is a myth. (D) Single men make up a small percentage of those persons who are counted among the poor. (E) Latinos are also disproportionately represented among the poor, but not in total numbers.

95. **(C)**   Stereotypes are false generalizations made about individuals because of the group they belong to. (A) Prejudice are preconceived ideas about others. (B) Discrimination is differential treatment group membership. (D) The authoritarian personality is a theory explaining the development of prejudice. (E) Scapegoating is the process of seeking others to place blame for our own sense of inferiority.

96. **(D)**   Urbanization is the growth in the size and influence of cities. (A) Gentrification is the process of revitalizing aging city neighborhoods. (B) Suburbanization is the process of expanding suburban communities. (C) Rural renaissance is the reemergence of rural areas. (E) Incumbent upgrading is when residents improve the housing in their neighborhood.

97. **(A)**   While many men are now doing housework, in most families the women still have the primary responsibility for the home even when they work outside the home. (B) Women do not have more second jobs when compared to men. (C) Women work similar time patterns to men. (D) This is no longer true. In many families, the wife's income is a sub-

stantial proportion of the family income. (E) There are still substantial differences in earnings for comparable work.

98. **(C)** Cultural universals are social patterns that are present in all societies (e.g., family). (A) Norms are expectations we have of each other. They vary from culture to culture. (B) Folkways are the everyday customs of a people. (D) Laws exist in historical societies, but do not exist in prehistoric societies. (E) Fashions are norms that last for a relatively short period of time.

99. **(D)** Ideal types are models used in the analysis of social organizations. (A) Theories are attempts at explanation. (B) A construct is a complex of impressions or images. (C) Concepts are concretized ideas. (E) Variables are characteristics that vary from group to group.

100. **(B)** Structural mobility is due to changes in the labor market whereby low level jobs disappear and higher level jobs are created. (A) Immigrants do not play a role in the question. (C) Because of his promotion, Louis is not experiencing downward mobility. (D) This is not individual mobility because Louis did not achieve this change because of his personal initiative. (E) The promotion precludes the horizontal mobility answer.

▼

PRACTICE
TEST 3

CLEP INTRODUCTORY SOCIOLOGY
Test 3

(Answer sheets appear in the back of this book.)

TIME: 90 Minutes
100 Questions

DIRECTIONS: Each of the questions or incomplete statements below is followed by five possible answers or completions. Select the best choice in each case and fill in the corresponding oval on the answer sheet.

---

1. Sociology is best defined as the scientific study of

   (A) social problems.

   (B) human personality.

   (C) social interaction.

   (D) human development.

   (E) attitudes and values.

2. Sociology developed as a separate discipline in the nineteenth century in response to

   (A) the growth of socialism.

   (B) the spread of colonialism.

   (C) a desire to promote greater equality.

   (D) the growth of industrial society.

   (E) disenchantment with psychology.

3. The German sociologist Max Weber is best known for his study

   (A) *Street Corner Society.*

   (B) *The Division of Labor in Society.*

(C) *The Human Group.*

(D) *The Protestant Ethic and the Spirit of Capitalism.*

(E) *The Theory of the Leisure Class.*

4. In his writings, the French sociologist Emile Durkheim placed great emphasis on the concept of

(A) class conflict.

(B) social solidarity.

(C) rationalization.

(D) social mobility.

(E) reference groups.

5. In his theory, Karl Marx explained that conflict between industrial workers and the owners of industry was

(A) likely to decline in future years.

(B) usually harmful to social institutions.

(C) an inevitable consequence of capitalism.

(D) of little importance to social change.

(E) a rare occurrence in modern societies.

6. The research method that relies on interviews with a randomly selected sample of people is known as

(A) survey research.

(B) participant observation.

(C) content analysis.

(D) experimentation.

(E) exploratory research.

7. "Birth rates are lower in nations with high levels of economic development." This statement is an example of a

(A) positive correlation.

(B) spurious correlation.

(C) circular correlation.

(D) negative correlation.

(E) reverse correlation.

8. Which of the following concepts is most clearly at the core of the sociological theory known as functionalism?

(A) Economic development   (B) Class conflict

(C) Human communication   (D) Intellectual creativity

(E) Interdependence

9.   Which of the following is an example of upward social mobility?

(A) A farm worker's son becomes president of the U.S.

(B) A physician's daughter attends medical school

(C) A college professor's son works as a truck driver

(D) The daughter of an army officer joins the navy

(E) The son of a banker becomes a poet

10.   Which of the following is most frequently used by sociologists as a measure of a person's socioeconomic status in industrial societies?

(A) The prestige of their occupation

(B) The amount of leisure time they possess

(C) The number of children they have

(D) Their participation in politics

(E) Their religious beliefs

11.   For sociologists, the key feature of a middle class family that distinguishes it from a working class family is the

(A) head of the middle class family works at more than one job.

(B) wife of the middle class family is a full-time homemaker.

(C) children in the middle class family attend private schools.

(D) workers in the middle class family hold white-collar occupations.

(E) middle class family owns more cars and more expensive homes.

12.   Sociological research in the United States has found all of the following EXCEPT

(A) middle class people attend church more often than lower class people.

(B) lower class people are ill more frequently than middle class people.

(C) middle class parents use physical punishment less often than lower class parents.

(D) lower class people are less involved in politics than middle class people.

(E) lower class families have fewer children than middle class families.

13. Since 1989, the number of poor people in the United States has

(A) remained the same.

(B) steadily increased.

(C) reached an all-time low.

(D) steadily decreased.

(E) increased in some years, decreased in others.

14. Many young people around the world now wear American blue jeans and listen to American rock and roll music. This is an example of the concept of cultural

(A) decline.   (D) innovation.

(B) diffusion.   (E) disintegration.

(C) discovery.

15. Popular movies frequently portray young African-American men as gang members and drug dealers. This is an example of the sociological process known as

(A) affirmative action.   (D) status inconsistency.

(B) reverse racism.   (E) role conflict.

(C) stereotyping.

16. According to the functionalist theory of stratification developed by Kingsley Davis and Wilbert Moore, some occupations are more highly rewarded than others because they

(A) have been held for a long time.

(B) are organized into unions.

(C) require physical labor.

(D) appeal to widely shared values.

(E) require long periods of training.

17. Demographers study all of the following aspects of human populations EXCEPT

(A) growth.   (D) composition.

(B) distribution.   (E) socialization.

(C) migration.

18. Each of the following is an important agent of socialization EXCEPT

(A) television.   (D) peers.

(B) bankers.   (E) teachers.

(C) parents.

19. Emile Durkheim found that suicide rates were higher for

(A) women than men.

(B) young people than old people.

(C) poor people than wealthy people.

(D) single people than married people.

(E) Jews than Protestants.

20. A soldier in combat sacrifices his life so his comrades may survive. This is an example of which of the following types of suicide identified by Durkheim?

(A) Egoistic   (D) Anomic

(B) Altruistic   (E) Euphoric

(C) Intrinsic

21. The research method which involves a social scientist living among and interacting with the people being studied is known as

(A) survey research.   (B) experimentation.

(C) content analysis.   (D) participant observation.

(E) strategic engagement.

22. "Female college athletes will have higher academic averages than male college athletes." In this hypothesis, which is the independent variable?

(A) Athletic participation   (D) Gender

(B) College attendance   (E) Study habits

(C) Academic achievement

23. The concept of culture includes all of the following EXCEPT

(A) personal values.   (D) family organization.

(B) religious beliefs.   (E) individual intelligence.

(C) styles of dress.

24. The concept of ethnocentrism refers to the tendency for members of a group to

(A) speak the same language.

(B) work for common goals.

(C) show respect for the elderly.

(D) teach children to practice religious rituals.

(E) place a high value on their own culture.

25. According to sociologists, an important difference between folkways and mores is that

(A) violation of a folkway leads to severe punishment.

(B) mores are found among the upper classes only.

(C) folkways include customary behaviors.

(D) violations of mores are not considered crimes.

(E) folkways apply to sexual behavior only.

26. Deviant behavior is the term used by sociologists to describe behaviors which a group defines as

    (A) violating basic norms.

    (B) uncommonly brave or heroic.

    (C) the standard for others to follow.

    (D) very rare or unusual.

    (E) based on personal motives.

27. Which of the following behaviors would NOT be considered an example of deviance in contemporary American society?

    (A) Eating spaghetti with one's fingers

    (B) Running naked down a main street of a city

    (C) A man regularly dressing in women's clothing

    (D) College students drinking beer on Saturday night

    (E) A person talking to himself in public places

28. According to the symbolic interactionist theory of George Herbert Mead, which of the following processes is central to the development of a self-concept by young children?

    (A) Pretending to be other people

    (B) Memorizing songs and poems

    (C) Learning how to read in school

    (D) Listening to bedtime stories

    (E) Saying prayers in church

29. Studies of children who have been raised with limited contact with other humans during their first years have shown that they

    (A) develop intellectually at a normal rate.

    (B) have better coordination than other children.

    (C) have great difficulty adjusting to society.

    (D) easily learn to distinguish right and wrong.

    (E) often show considerable artistic talent.

30. All of the following are basic assumptions of sociology EXCEPT

    (A) most human behavior follows predictable patterns.

    (B) scientific methods can be used to study human behavior.

    (C) inherited genetic traits shape much human behavior.

    (D) human beliefs and values can be studied objectively.

    (E) human values are acquired through socialization.

31. "Working class mothers will place a higher value on obedience in raising their children than will middle class mothers." In this hypothesis, which is the dependent variable?

    (A) Social class of mothers   (D) Education of parents

    (B) Gender of children   (E) Social status of mothers

    (C) Value placed on obedience

32. Which of the following is NOT a method of social control?

    (A) Ridicule   (D) Praise

    (B) Insults   (E) Imitation

    (C) Spanking

33. George is a college student. He also works 25 hours a week to support his wife and small child. He is having a hard time pleasing his boss and keeping his grades up. A sociologist would say that George is suffering from

    (A) role ambiguity.   (D) role performance.

    (B) role conflict.   (E) role playing.

    (C) role strain.

34. Which of the following is an ascribed status?

    (A) College president   (D) White female

    (B) Nobel prize winner   (E) Opera singer

    (C) Honor student

35. Which of the following is an achieved status?

    (A) Television game show host

    (B) Senior citizen

    (C) Japanese-American teenager

    (D) Accident victim

    (E) Seven feet tall

36. If a group is considered a subculture by sociologists, then the people in that group would be most likely to have similar

    (A) values.   (D) ages.

    (B) incomes.   (E) genders.

    (C) educations.

37. "Our self-concept is based largely on the ways in which we see other people reacting to us." This statement reflects

    (A) George Herbert Mead's theory of self-development.

    (B) Charles Cooley's theory of the "looking-glass self."

    (C) Sigmund Freud's theory of ego development.

    (D) Jean Piaget's theory of intellectual development.

    (E) Lawrence Kohlberg's theory of moral development.

38. Sociologists have identified at least five different types of societies based on their level of sociocultural evolution. Hunting and gathering societies differ from other types of societies in that they have

    (A) more rigid social stratification.

    (B) greater occupational specialization.

    (C) extensive inequality of wealth.

    (D) stronger consensus on basic values.

    (E) a highly centralized government.

39. Which one of the following statements about poverty in the United States is correct?

    (A) The majority of African-Americans are poor.

    (B) The majority of elderly are poor.

    (C) The majority of the poor are whites.

    (D) The majority of the poor are African-Americans.

    (E) The majority of the poor are single mothers.

40. Social mobility refers to the ability to

    (A) gain a college education.

    (B) enter any occupation one chooses.

    (C) travel freely across national borders.

    (D) change one's social class position.

    (E) marry a person of another religion.

41. When sociologists discuss the working class they are referring to people who

    (A) work for a living.

    (B) live below the poverty line.

    (C) have not attended college.

    (D) work in blue-collar occupations.

    (E) live near factories.

42. When sociologists use the term ethnic group, they are referring to people who have

    (A) a shared cultural heritage.

    (B) low social status.

    (C) similar physical appearance.

    (D) common political views.

    (E) the same occupation.

43. The concept of prejudice is defined as

    (A) belief in the superiority of one's group.

    (B) negative attitudes towards another group.

    (C) harmful behavior toward minority groups.

    (D) blaming another group for one's problems.

    (E) inability to improve one's social status.

44. One distinctive feature of the Indian caste system is

    (A) women generally have higher status than men.

    (B) individual mobility between castes rarely occurs.

    (C) lower castes have considerable wealth.

    (D) status is based on one's level of education.

    (E) there is much intermarriage between castes.

45. A minority group is defined as a group of people who

    (A) usually vote for the same political party.

    (B) have high levels of income and education.

    (C) have experienced prejudice and discrimination.

    (D) practice the same religious rituals.

    (E) send their children to private schools.

46. Max Weber first discussed the essential characteristics of bureau-cracy. One of these is

    (A) equal authority among members of the organization.

    (B) group participation in important decisions.

    (C) workers develop skills at a variety of tasks.

    (D) a clearly defined chain of command.

    (E) maximum flexibility in interpreting rules.

47. When studying leadership in small groups, Robert Bales discovered that most groups have two types of leaders. These are

    (A) instrumental and expressive.

    (B) rigid and flexible.

    (C) forceful and timid.

    (D) participatory and consultative.

    (E) demonstrative and reserved.

48. Sociologists who have studied industrial corporations in Japan have identified several differences between Japanese and American companies. One of these is

    (A) Japanese workers are better paid.

    (B) American workers work longer hours.

    (C) Japanese workers have less job security.

    (D) American workers are more loyal to their employers.

    (E) Japanese workers take part in more group activities.

49. Sociologists have identified several essential characteristics of social groups. All of the following are important characteristics of a group EXCEPT

    (A) regular interaction among members.

    (B) shared norms and values.

    (C) members identify with the group.

    (D) some specialization of roles.

    (E) absence of conflict among members.

50. Sociologists use the term voluntary association to refer to an organization which

    (A) is organized to make a profit.

    (B) engages in retail sales.

    (C) selects new members on the basis of merit.

    (D) has an authoritarian form of government.

    (E) members join to pursue common interests.

51. Which of the following terms would be an accurate description of family and kinship practices that are most prominent in the United States today?

I. Matrilineal descent system

II. Nuclear family

III. Neolocal family

IV. Matriarchal family

(A) I only.

(B) I and II only.

(C) I, II, and III only.

(D) I and III only.

(E) II and III only.

52. Which of the following sociological theorists argues that religion as a social institution tends to protect the status quo by encouraging less powerful groups toward a "false class consciousness," or a misunderstanding of what policies and practices would be in their true interests?

(A) Karl Marx

(B) Robert Bellah

(C) Emile Durkheim

(D) Max Weber

(E) Robert Michels

53. In studying schools in modern societies, conflict theorists point to a "hidden curriculum." This term refers to

(A) those parts of school budgets that are not made public.

(B) the passing on of values and norms in school that perpetuate the existing system of stratification.

(C) those parts of the curriculum that parents are not aware of.

(D) that proportion of the student body that drops out of school before graduating each year.

(E) those parts of the school budget that are used for things other than direct student instruction.

54. Some parts of the political system in the United States utilize laws and bureaucratic rules to define who has what kind of power and authority over whom. These laws and rules exemplify which type of authority?

    (A) Traditional
    (B) Charismatic
    (C) Legal-rational
    (D) Institutionalized
    (E) Corporate

55. Which of the following statements best characterizes the trends in the economy of the United States over the past few decades?

    (A) The extent of corporate concentration has declined.

    (B) Market forces have become a less powerful determinant of the production and distribution of goods.

    (C) The power elite is now concentrated more in the political sphere than the economic.

    (D) Union membership has declined steadily as a percentage of the entire work force.

    (E) The industrial sector has grown as a proportion of the overall economy.

56. Which of the following would be considered characteristics of a caste stratification system?

    I.   Rigid boundaries between classes

    II. Rank is based on heredity

    III. Achieved statuses predominate

    (A) I only.
    (B) I and II only.
    (C) II only.
    (D) II and III only.
    (E) I, II, and III.

57. Which of the following provides the best illustration of intra-generational social mobility?

   (A) Chris joined the ABC publishing corporation as a traveling sales representative and was promoted over the years to the position of senior vice president of the corporation.

   (B) Mary's mother is a neurosurgeon, and Mary goes to medical school and becomes a cardiac surgeon.

   (C) Fred works as a carpenter for the ABC construction company and then takes a job as a carpenter for the XYZ construction company because the pay is better.

   (D) Nancy worked as a nurse in a large hospital but quit so that she could stay at home and raise her new infant.

   (E) Tom's father is a grade school teacher, and Tom becomes a high school teacher after graduating from college.

58. Which of the following statements would be most consistent with the approach of conflict theory to the explanation of social stratification and social inequality?

   (A) Social inequality persists because it works to motivate people to make a contribution to society.

   (B) Social stratification persists because it benefits all groups in society by providing a wider distribution of resources.

   (C) Social inequality persists because the well-to-do use their monopoly over resources to dominate and exploit those with less resources.

   (D) Social inequality persists mostly because the poor will not expend the amount of work necessary to improve their circumstances.

   (E) Social stratification persists because it is a rational system for distributing resources.

59. In south Florida, Hispanics and Anglos live together but have each retained a distinct identity and lifestyle. The former continue to speak Spanish and keep much of their Caribbean, Cuban, or South American heritage, while the latter speak English and retain the European heritage. This best illustrates

   (A) pluralism.   (B) assimilation.

(C) segregation.   (D) separatism.

(E) submission.

60. A group is called a minority group by sociologists when it

(A) is denied access to power and resources available to other groups.

(B) consists of less than one-half the total population in a society.

(C) consists of less than one-tenth the total population in a society.

(D) wields power in society even though it has few numbers.

(E) has recently immigrated to a particular society.

61. Generally speaking, prejudice and discrimination would be most likely to occur between two racial or ethnic groups under which of the following conditions?

(A) The two groups work together to achieve common goals.

(B) Contact between the two groups involves group members of roughly equal status getting to know one another.

(C) Members of the two groups compete for the same scarce jobs.

(D) One group has been completely assimilated into the other group.

(E) Members of both groups are able to find jobs that pay comparable wages.

62. Which of the following is a social policy aimed especially at reducing the disparities in income between men and women?

(A) Feminism   (D) Androgyny

(B) Sexism   (E) Separatism

(C) Comparable worth

63. Since 1900 in the United States, which occupational groups have been growing as a percentage of the work force?

I.   White-collar workers

II. Blue-collar workers

III. Service workers

IV. Farm workers

(A) I only.   (D) I and III only.

(B) I and II only.   (E) II and III only.

(C) I, II, and III only.

64. In the study of population, the three elements that most directly determine the size, composition, and distribution of a population are

(A) fertility, mortality, and migration.

(B) fertility, mortality, and community.

(C) fertility, migration, and fecundity.

(D) mortality, migration, and segregation.

(E) fertility, mortality, and ecology.

65. In terms of controlling population growth in societies around the world, which of the following statements is true regarding the effects of various factors on birth rates?

(A) Family planning programs actually lead to overall increases in birth rates.

(B) Rising birth rates are associated with increases in urbanization.

(C) Economic development results in declines in birth rates.

(D) Greater gender equality results in a higher birth rate.

(E) Patriarchal family systems have lower birth rates than egalitarian ones.

66. Which of the following terms would be most clearly linked with the kind of social life and social interaction found in cities rather than rural communities?

(A) *Gemeinschaft*   (D) *Verstehen*

(B) In-group   (E) *Gesellschaft*

(C) Groupthink

67. Which of the following is the best example of a social aggregate?

(A) Thirteen people riding in a subway car, each reading or staring out the window

(B) Twelve jurors listening to testimony in a courtroom

(C) Eleven members of a college football team executing a play on the field

(D) All African-American females attending a particular university

(E) The two parents and three children that constitute a particular nuclear family

68. When a person interacts with his or her best friend, the group they form would most likely constitute which kind of group?

(A) A secondary group

(B) An out-group

(C) A primary group

(D) A postindustrial group

(E) A formal group

69. John is introduced to Fred, and the two of them shake hands. This hand-shaking ritual is best characterized as a

(A) more.

(B) taboo.

(C) law.

(D) folkway.

(E) sanction.

70. Which of the following theories of deviant behavior is based on the symbolic interactionist perspective in sociology?

(A) Sutherland's differential association theory

(B) Merton's anomie theory

(C) Park's concentric-zone theory

(D) Lombroso's body-type theory

(E) Hoyt's sector theory

71. Fans at a rock concert respond to the music and mood by raucous shouting and screaming, dancing with one another in the aisle and in front of the stage, and throwing flowers onto the stage. These fans would be best characterized as

(A) an acting crowd.

(B) a casual crowd.

(C) an expressive crowd.

(D) a rioting crowd.

(E) mass hysteria.

72. When English and Spanish explorers in the 1500s found Indians in the Americas using tobacco, they brought the tobacco back to Europe. After this introduction, the use of tobacco spread throughout Europe. The beginning of the use of tobacco in Europe is most accurately an example of

(A) invention.

(D) revolution.

(B) diffusion.

(E) discovery.

(C) cultural lag.

73. Which of the following people is considered the founder of the field of sociology and is credited with first using the word "sociology"?

(A) Emile Durkheim

(D) Auguste Comte

(B) Talcott Parsons

(E) Herbert Spencer

(C) Karl Marx

74. If a sociologist wished to collect data from a random sample of 1,500 people spread across the United States, it would be most feasible to use which type of research method?

(A) A survey

(D) Unobtrusive measures

(B) Participant observation

(E) A laboratory experiment

(C) Face-to-face interviews

75. Which of the following statements would be most consistent with social exchange theory in sociology?

(A) Society consists of many interrelated and interdependent parts, each contributing to the maintenance of society.

(B) People interpret reality and act on the basis of their definition of the situation.

(C) People weigh the benefits and costs of various lines of action before deciding how to act in a situation.

(D) Competition, conflict, and dominance and subordination are inherent features of the social system.

(E) A society tends toward relative stability or dynamic equilibrium.

76. The "power-elite" theory of government contends all of the following groups hold power in the United States EXCEPT

    (A) the wealthy.

    (B) corporations.

    (C) citizens.

    (D) political leaders.

    (E) All of the above.

77. Mike, who is married to Sarah, decides to also marry Beth. The term used to describe this type of marriage is

    (A) polyandry.

    (B) polygamy.

    (C) monogamy.

    (D) orgy.

    (E) cult.

78. Lorraine and Bob get married and move near the bride's parents. The phrase that best describes this situation is

    (A) matrilocal residence.

    (B) patrilocal residence.

    (C) matrilineal.

    (D) monogamy.

    (E) polygamy.

79. _____ is the practice of placing students into groups which receive different treatment on the basis of their assumed similarity in ability.

    (A) Social mobility

    (B) Cultural capital

    (C) Socialization

    (D) Tracking

    (E) None of the above.

80. "Cultural Capital," a concept coined by Pierre Bourdieu, is defined as

    (A) the process by which one's self-concept is formed through the responses of others.

    (B) the process of mentally assuming the role of another.

    (C) the cultural benefits and advantages passed on to succeeding generations.

    (D) seeing one's own culture as superior to others.

    (E) a culture within a culture.

81. Martha owns a paint store in a predominantly Korean neighborhood. Bill, who is white, asks Martha for a summer job. Although Martha is not prejudiced herself, she declines, for fear that other Koreans in the neighborhood will refuse to buy their paint at a store where a white man works. Martha can be defined as

    (A) an "all-weather liberal" (non-prejudiced, non-discriminator).

    (B) an "all-weather bigot" (prejudiced, discriminator).

    (C) a "timid bigot" (prejudiced, non-discriminator).

    (D) a "fair-weather liberal" (non-prejudiced, discriminator).

    (E) None of the above.

82. Denzel, one of Santa's elves, is born into a society where his only purpose is to take care of the reindeer. He wants desperately to make toys because toy-making has the highest status. No matter how hard he tries, however, he cannot elevate to toy-maker because making toys is reserved for Santa's offspring. This society can be classified as a

    (A) class system.   (D) socialist system.

    (B) colonial system.   (E) None of the above.

    (C) caste system.

83. The phrase _____ best sums up the idea of "meritocracy."

    (A) "hanging out with bad apples will make you a bad apple"

    (B) "you get what you work for"

    (C) "from each according to his abilities, to each according to his need"

    (D) "hard work is irrelevant to what you achieve in life"

    (E) None of the above.

84. During the course of their working lives, about _____ percent of women are affected by some form of sexual harassment.

    (A) 5   (D) 50

    (B) 10   (E) 70

    (C) 25

85. Studies on the "underclass" have refuted which of the following myths about living in poverty?

    (A) Most welfare recipients are able-bodied adults.

    (B) Most welfare mothers have many children.

    (C) People who live in poverty could find work if they wanted to.

    (D) People who are poor do not value hard work.

    (E) All of the above.

86. Which of the following terms refers to thinking in fixed, inflexible categories?

    (A) Stereotyping   (D) Discrimination

    (B) Selective perception (E) None of the above.

    (C) Scapegoating

87. Social stratification is functionally necessary according to Davis and Moore. The rank of an occupation within the stratification system, according to these theorists, is determined by what factors?

    (A) How prestigious the job is according to members of the society.

    (B) Where the job lies with respect to the means of production.

    (C) The amount of training and aptitude required to do the job, as well as how important the job is to society.

    (D) How much physical risk is involved in performing the job.

    (E) All of the above.

88. While _____ is an action or behavior directed at a particular group, _____ refers to the attitude or belief held about this group.

    (A) discrimination; ageism

    (B) scapegoating; racism

    (C) ethnocentricism; prejudice

    (D) discrimination; prejudice

    (E) None of the above.

89. Which of the following landmark Supreme Court decisions outlawed public school segregation in 1954, leading to the fear of integration among many urban whites?

    (A) *Brown v. Board of Education of Topeka*

    (B) *Roe v. Wade*

    (C) *Plessy v. Ferguson*

    (D) *Bakke v. University of California*

    (E) None of the above.

90. The phrase _____ refers to the maximum number of years that an individual can live.

    (A) crude death rate

    (B) infant mortality rate

    (C) life expectancy

    (D) life span

    (E) None of the above.

91. According to Immanuel Wallerstein's World Systems Theory, which of the following countries is not in the core?

    (A) United States

    (B) Ireland

    (C) Japan

    (D) Germany

    (E) All of the above are core countries.

92. Regarding theories of deviance, the idea that an individual commits deviant acts because he "hangs out with the wrong crowd" follows what line of thinking?

    (A) Cultural association

    (B) Strain theory

    (C) Labeling theory

    (D) Control theory

    (E) None of the above.

93. According to Jack Gibbs's Deterrence Theory, the crime rate will decrease if punishments are all of the following EXCEPT

    (A) severe.

    (B) swift.

(C) long-lasting.   (D) certain.

(E) All of the above.

94. While _____ are established standards of behavior, _____
     legitimate them.

     (A) roles; values   (D) mores; cultures

     (B) cultures; norms   (E) norms; values

     (C) roles; statuses

95. Which of the following statements best describes Cooley's notion of
     the "looking-glass-self"?

     (A) How we think of ourselves depends on how influential people,
          like parents, think of us.

     (B) How we think of others is based on how we think of ourselves.

     (C) Our self-concept is formed by observing others' responses to us.

     (D) Our self-concept is determined by our genetic make-up.

     (E) None of the above.

96. All of the people riding the escalator at the mall form a/an

     (A) aggregate.   (D) primary group.

     (B) secondary group.   (E) coalition.

     (C) social category.

97. For her experiment on drinking behavior, Lynn wants a control group
     and an experimental group. If she knew all of the variables that may
     influence drinking behavior, she could try to match people. By using
     a procedure called _____, however, she can assume the two
     groups will be alike.

     (A) participant observation   (D) unobtrusive measure

     (B) convenience sample   (E) random assignment

     (C) reliability

98. G. H. Mead's concept of "taking the role of the other" refers to

    (A) viewing a person in terms of how they would view themselves.

    (B) being persuaded to take on a role previously held by another.

    (C) learning to mimic our parents and other members of our primary group.

    (D) the process of mentally assuming the perspective of another.

    (E) None of the above.

99. Bob was a member of the Branch Davidian cult in Waco, Texas. After a confrontation with the federal government, he and the other members decide to commit suicide by lighting themselves on fire. This type of suicide can be referred to as

    (A) altruistic.   (D) fatalistic.

    (B) egoistic.   (E) None of the above.

    (C) anomic.

100. Jane wants to survey all Jewish men who are registered Republican in the state of New Jersey. Because she cannot interview all of them, the desirable alternative is to

    (A) survey a few that live in her neighborhood.

    (B) survey those who attend a local synagogue.

    (C) survey a random sample of the total population.

    (D) interview Jewish male Republicans who agree to be questioned.

    (E) None of the above.

CLEP INTRODUCTORY SOCIOLOGY
TEST 3

ANSWER KEY

1.	(C)	26.	(A)	51.	(E)	76.	(C)
2.	(D)	27.	(D)	52.	(A)	77.	(B)
3.	(D)	28.	(A)	53.	(B)	78.	(A)
4.	(B)	29.	(C)	54.	(C)	79.	(D)
5.	(C)	30.	(C)	55.	(D)	80.	(C)
6.	(A)	31.	(C)	56.	(B)	81.	(D)
7.	(D)	32.	(E)	57.	(A)	82.	(C)
8.	(E)	33.	(B)	58.	(C)	83.	(B)
9.	(A)	34.	(D)	59.	(A)	84.	(E)
10.	(A)	35.	(A)	60.	(A)	85.	(E)
11.	(D)	36.	(A)	61.	(C)	86.	(A)
12.	(E)	37.	(B)	62.	(C)	87.	(C)
13.	(B)	38.	(D)	63.	(D)	88.	(D)
14.	(B)	39.	(C)	64.	(A)	89.	(A)
15.	(C)	40.	(D)	65.	(C)	90.	(D)
16.	(E)	41.	(D)	66.	(E)	91.	(B)
17.	(E)	42.	(A)	67.	(A)	92.	(A)
18.	(B)	43.	(B)	68.	(C)	93.	(C)
19.	(D)	44.	(B)	69.	(D)	94.	(E)
20.	(B)	45.	(C)	70.	(A)	95.	(C)
21.	(D)	46.	(D)	71.	(C)	96.	(A)
22.	(D)	47.	(A)	72.	(B)	97.	(E)
23.	(E)	48.	(E)	73.	(D)	98.	(D)
24.	(E)	49.	(E)	74.	(A)	99.	(A)
25.	(C)	50.	(E)	75.	(C)	100.	(C)

DETAILED EXPLANATIONS OF ANSWERS

TEST 3

1.   **(C)**   Sociology studies human interaction, both in small groups and in larger settings, and the results of that interaction, such as groups, organizations, institutions, and nations. Social problems (A) are only a part of the subject matter of sociology. Human personality (B) and human development (D) are more often studied by psychologists. Attitudes and values (E) are only a part of the subject matter of sociology.

2.   **(D)**   The Industrial Revolution in Europe brought about the decline of traditional agricultural societies and the rapid growth of cities. The social dislocations that resulted from this change stimulated thinkers to consider the nature of social order and social change, and the outcome was the emergence of sociology as a separate discipline. Socialism (A) was another result of this change, but socialism as a movement for political change was separate from the discipline of sociology. (B) is incorrect because early sociologists were little concerned about the spread of colonialism during this period. While the founders of sociology were interested in the study of social inequality, they did little to promote greater equality; therefore, (C) is incorrect. (E) is incorrect because psychology developed as a separate discipline somewhat later than sociology.

3.   **(D)**   In *The Protestant Ethic and the Spirit of Capitalism* Weber studied the influence of the religious changes of the Reformation on the growth of capitalism in Europe. *Street Corner Society* (A) is by William F. Whyte. *The Division of Labor in Society* (B) is by Emile Durkheim. *The Human Group* (C) is by George C. Homans. *The Theory of the Leisure Class* (E) is by Thorstein Veblen.

4.   **(B)**   In his study of suicide, Durkheim explained how the decline of social solidarity in modern society has led to the growth of anomie

(normlessness) and associated social problems such as suicide. Class conflict (A) is most closely associated with the work of Karl Marx. Rationalization (C) is most closely associated with the work of Max Weber. (D) is incorrect because Durkheim devoted relatively little attention to social mobility. The theory of reference groups (E) was developed long after Durkheim's death.

5.   **(C)**   Marx concluded that conflict between workers and owners was an intrinsic feature of capitalist societies. Since Marx saw this conflict as the principal reason for social change, (D) is incorrect. He also believed this conflict would intensify over time and result in a socialist revolution, so (A) is also incorrect.   (B) is incorrect because Marx felt this conflict would ultimately benefit society instead of harming it.

6.   **(A)**   Survey research is based on data gathered by personal interviews or written questionnaires administered to a random sample of a larger population. Participant observation (B) involves observing people interacting in natural settings. Content analysis (C) involves the analysis of the content of communications, such as television advertising, letters, or text books. Experimentation (D) involves manipulation of an experimental stimulus on an experimental group and withholding that stimulus from a control group. Exploratory research (E) employs no specific methodology.

7.   **(D)**   A statistical relationship in which high values in one variable (economic development) are associated with low values in another variable (birth rate) is known as a negative or inverse correlation. Plotting the data points on a graph would produce a line with a downward (negative) slope. A positive correlation (A) is one in which high values in one variable are associated with high values in another variable. A spurious correlation (B) is one in which the apparent relationship between two variables is really due to a third variable. There is no such thing as a circular correlation (C) or a reverse correlation (E).

8.   **(E)**   Functionalism stresses the interdependence among parts of a society, pointing out how changes in one part of a social system will have consequences for other parts of that system. Economic development (A), class conflict (B), human communication (C), and intellectual creativity (D) are found in all human societies, but are not especially stressed in functionalist theory.

9.   **(A)**   Upward social mobility involves an individual improving his or her social status, i.e., moving from a lower class to a higher class. Going from a farm worker's home to the White House involves considerable upward mobility. The other examples involve children staying at the same status as their parents' or, in the case of the professor's son, downward mobility.

10.   **(A)**   The prestige of one's occupation is one of the most valid and reliable indicators of a person's status in industrial societies. Of course, there are exceptions, e.g., retired persons. The other answers may have some relation to social status, but none are as consistently or as strongly linked to a person's socioeconomic status.

11.   **(D)**   For sociologists, occupation is an essential feature that distinguishes the social classes. Working class individuals hold blue-collar jobs. Middle class individuals hold white-collar jobs. The other choices may be true of some middle class families, but they would not be true of all.

12.   **(E)**   Birth rates tend to be higher in lower class families than in other social classes. All of the other statements are supported by research findings.

13.   **(B)**   Since 1989 the number of poor people, as reported by the Census Bureau, has increased each year—from 31.9 million in 1989 to 39.3 million in 1993. The numbers have not declined in any of these years.

14.   **(B)**   Cultural diffusion is the spread of an idea, a fashion, or a technology from one culture to another. Blue jeans and rock and roll music originated in the United States and have now spread to most other nations of the world. Cultural discovery (C) and cultural innovation (D) imply the appearance of something unique or original. Cultural decline (A) and cultural disintegration (E) imply the destruction of previous cultural traits.

15.   **(C)**   A stereotype is a simplified image of personal characteristics (usually negative) which is applied to all members of a group. Affirmative action (A) involves giving preference or special consideration to members of minority groups. Reverse racism (B) involves discrimination against members of dominant or majority groups. Status inconsistency (D) refers to individuals who rank highly in one measure of social status and low in

another (e.g., a Ph.D. who drives a taxi). Role conflict (E) refers to individuals who occupy multiple roles with contradictory expectations.

16. **(E)** Davis and Moore hypothesized that high rewards are necessary to motivate individuals to complete the long periods of training required for some occupations, such as physician. This theory does not consider factors such as seniority (A), unionization (B), physical labor (C), or appeal to values (D).

17. **(E)** Demography is the study of the growth (A), composition (D), distribution (B), and migration (C) of human populations. Socialization is not usually studied by demographers.

18. **(B)** Agents of socialization teach social norms and values to children and adults. Parents (C), peers (D), and teachers (E) impart social norms directly to young people. Television (A) is also an important medium for teaching norms and values. Occupations such as banking do not involve the teaching of norms and values as part of their primary responsibilities.

19. **(D)** Durkheim found that people with few social attachments (i.e., single people) tend to commit suicide more frequently. Men (A), old people (B), wealthy people (C), and Protestants (E) all have lower suicide rates.

20. **(B)** Durkheim used the term altruistic suicide to refer to people who commit suicide because of their intense sense of loyalty to a group. Egoistic suicide (A) refers to people who kill themselves for selfish, personal reasons. Anomic suicide (D) refers to people killing themselves because they lack clear moral guidelines. Intrinsic suicide (C) and euphoric suicide (E) are not terms that Durkheim used.

21. **(D)** Participant observation involves a researcher interacting with and observing the personal lives of the research subjects. Survey research (A) gathers data from subjects using questionnaires or interviews. Experimentation (B) involves a researcher manipulating an experimental stimulus, usually in a laboratory setting. Content analysis (C) involves the study of communication products such as books, letters, advertising, or television programs. Strategic engagement (E) is not a method used in social research.

22. **(D)** The independent variable produces an effect or change in the dependent variable. In this case, gender is hypothesized to cause a difference in academic averages. Athletic participation (A) and college attendance (B) are not variables in this hypothesis since they are the same for both groups. Academic achievement (C) is the dependent variable. Study habits (E) may help to explain the difference between men and women, but it has not been stated in this hypothesis.

23. **(E)** Culture consists of the shared products of human interaction, both material and non-material. An individual's intelligence is the result of personal development and genetic inheritance. Because intelligence may vary greatly among individuals, it is not shared among members of a society.

24. **(E)** Ethnocentrism is the practice of placing a high value on one's own culture and demeaning all cultures that differ from it. Shared cultural traits such as language (A) and religion (D) do not constitute ethnocentrism. Working for common goals (B) and showing respect for the elderly (C) also have nothing to do with the concept of ethnocentrism.

25. **(C)** Folkways are social norms governing less important areas of behavior such as table manners or proper attire for events. Mores are social norms which concern more serious issues such as laws against murder or incest. (A) is incorrect since violations of folkways usually result in mild reprimands. (D) is incorrect because violations of mores are usually considered crimes and involve more drastic punishments. (B) and (E) are also incorrect because folkways and mores are found among all social groups and cover a wide range of behaviors.

26. **(A)** Deviance refers to those behaviors that a group stigmatizes because they are seen as violating basic norms. Rape, child abuse, and incest are examples of behaviors which are seen as deviant by many groups in the United States. Acts that are rare or unusual (D) are not considered deviant if they involve praiseworthy or inoffensive behaviors.

27. **(D)** In American society, social norms require that people eat spaghetti with a fork (A), wear gender appropriate clothing in public (C), and not talk to oneself (E). Beer drinking (D), however, is a normal activity among many American college students.

28.   **(A)**   Mead's theory of social development emphasizes the importance of children's play.   He maintains that they develop their self-concepts by imagining themselves in the roles of other people.   "Taking the role of the other" is central to his theory.

29.   **(C)**   Children who have been isolated from human contact do not learn basic social skills and values and, even with special help, have considerable difficulty functioning in society.   Their intellectual (A) and moral development (D) lags behind other children of the same age.   Unusual coordination (B) or artistic talents (E) have not been reported for these children.

30.   **(C)**   Sociologists believe that social conditions and processes, such as socialization (E), rather than genetic factors are the basic explanatory variables in human behavior.   They also assume human behavior follows predictable patterns (A) and that scientific methods (B) can be used to study these behaviors objectively (D).

31.   **(C)**   The dependent variable (value placed on obedience) may be influenced by the independent variable—social class of mothers (E).   Gender of children (B) and education of parents (D) are not mentioned in this hypothesis.   Social class (A) is the independent variable in this hypothesis.

32.   **(E)**   Verbal and physical rewards (D) and punishments, such as ridicule (A), insults (B), and spanking (C), are commonly used methods for enforcing conformity to social norms.   Imitation is not used to control the behavior of others.

33.   **(B)**   Role conflict is a situation where the multiple roles which an individual occupies place competing, and often contradictory, demands on his or her time and energy.   Role ambiguity (A) implies that role expectations are not clearly understood.   Role strain (C) refers to the excessive demands of a single role.   Role performance (D) and role playing (E) refer to the process of carrying out the expectations of a role.

34.   **(D)**   An ascribed status is one which an individual gains through no effort on his or her part.   Often one is born into an ascribed status.   Becoming a college president (A), a Nobel prize winner (B), an honor student (C), or an opera singer (E) all require considerable effort by an individual.   Being a white female is a condition over which one has no control.

35.   **(A)**   An achieved status is one which an individual receives through his or her own efforts. Categories based on age (B) or ethnic group (C) are ascribed, not achieved. Similarly, one has no control over one's height (E) or being an accident victim (D).

36.   **(A)**   A subculture is a distinctive lifestyle that exists within a larger culture. Members of the subculture share some values with the larger culture, but have other values that are unique to their group. People of the same income (B), education (C), age (D), or gender (E) do not necessarily share the same values.

37.   **(B)**   Cooley's theory of the "looking-glass self" maintains that our perceptions of others' actions toward us are a key factor in developing our self-concepts. Mead (A), Freud (C), Piaget (D), and Kohlberg (E) do not place similar emphasis on the individual's perceptions of other's reactions.

38.   **(D)**   Hunting and gathering societies are characterized by small size, low level of technology, equal status among adults, lack of strong authority figures, and consensus on values. There is little difference in wealth (C) or occupation (B) and no centralized government (E).

39.   **(C)**   While a higher percentage of African-Americans live in poverty (A), the largest number of poor people are white. While many single mothers (E) are poor, they are not a majority of poor Americans. The poverty rate for the elderly (B) is about the same as the national average—13 percent.

40.   **(D)**   Social mobility is movement to a higher (upward) or lower (downward) social status. Societies differ in the amount of social mobility that is possible for their members. The ability to gain an education (A) or enter an occupation (B) does not always lead to a change in status. Social mobility should not be confused with geographic mobility (C), moving across borders. It also has nothing to do with marriage to a person of another religion (E).

41.   **(D)**   The working class consists of people who hold manual, blue-collar jobs. Some may be highly skilled, such as electricians or tool makers, while others are unskilled laborers. Working class status is not based on one's education (C), residence (E), or income level (B).

42. **(A)** An ethnic group consists of people who share a common culture and sense of identity. While some ethnic groups are also minorities, others are not. An ethnic group often includes people of *different* social classes (B), occupations (E), and political views (D). Some, like Puerto Ricans and Cubans, include people with a variety of skin colors (C).

43. **(B)** Prejudice refers to preconceived negative attitudes towards people with distinctive social characteristics. It should not be confused with (A) ethnocentrism (belief in the superiority of one's own group), (C) discrimination (harmful behavior toward members of a minority group), or (D) scapegoating (blaming another group for one's problems). Prejudice may make it difficult for members of a minority group to improve their position (E).

44. **(B)** In the caste system one's status is determined at birth. Members of the upper castes usually enjoy greater wealth (C), though there are many exceptions. No amount of individual accomplishment, such as education (D), can raise or lower this caste position. Women (A) do not enjoy a higher position than men. Marriage between castes (E) is usually forbidden.

45. **(C)** The concept of minority group refers to people who share a low status in society, hold relatively little power, and are the object of prejudicial attitudes and discriminatory treatment. High levels of income or education (B) usually are not found in minority groups. Political preference (A) and type of schooling (E) have nothing to do with minority group status. While some minority groups share the same religion (D), others do not.

46. **(D)** Weber identified a hierarchical authority structure as a distinctive characteristic of bureaucracy. There is a well-defined chain of command which identifies who has authority in every aspect of the organization. Some members of the bureaucracy have greater authority (A) than others. Group decision making (B) is not usually found in bureaucracies. (C) and (E) are incorrect because specialization of tasks and rigid adherence to rules and regulations are other essential characteristics of bureaucracies.

47. **(A)** Bales found that small groups typically have one leader who directs it in accomplishing its goals (instrumental) and another who creates unity within the group and maintains harmony (expressive). The other choices refer to personal characteristics which may or may not be present in group leaders.

48. **(E)** Several researchers have reported a heavy emphasis on group activities, both on and off the job, for employees of Japanese corporations. (A) and (B) are incorrect because Japanese workers typically work longer hours for lower wages than American workers. Japanese workers actually enjoy *greater* job security (C) and demonstrate more loyalty (D) to their employers than their American counterparts.

49. **(E)** A group consists of members who regularly interact with each other (A). This interaction creates shared values (B), a sense of identity (C), and specialization of roles (D). There may be conflict among group members, but as long as they continue to interact with each other the group exists.

50. **(E)** A voluntary association is an organization like the League of Women Voters, Lions Club, or American Legion. Members typically join the organization because they wish to participate in its activities, not to earn an income (B) or make a profit (A). Selection of members (C) and type of government (D) vary greatly among voluntary organizations.

51. **(E)** Most families in the United States today are nuclear (consisting of a married couple and their children) and neolocal (residence tends to be separate from the families of either spouse). Choices (A), (B), (C), and (D) include either statement I or statement IV, both of which do not describe families in the United States today. A matrilineal system reckons descent through both male and female lines (bilateral); a matriarchal family is one in which women hold power and authority, but the United States is either patriarchal (men hold power) or egalitarian.

52. **(A)** Central to Marx's analysis of religion was its role in protecting the status quo by discouraging people from realizing that changing society would alleviate their troubles. Bellah (B) was a theorist of religion, but he focused on the type of religious organization that is found in different societies. Durkheim (C) was also a theorist on religion, but he took a functionalist approach, rather than the conflict perspective which underlies Marx's approach. Weber (D) was best known for his analysis of how religious beliefs can support economic institutions, such as capitalism. Michels (E), best known for his "iron law of oligarchy," theorized about political and economic institutions, not religion.

53. **(B)** The "hidden curriculum" refers to the ways, sometimes subtle and indirect, that schools teach students to support the status quo and its system of inequalities. (A), (C), (D), and (E) refer to aspects of the school budget, the curriculum, or the student body that, while they may have implications for the hidden curriculum or be related to it, are not a statement of what the hidden curriculum is.

54. **(C)** Legal-rational authority is the type of authority based on rules and laws. (A) and (B) are incorrect because they refer to other bases of authority, namely, authority based on customary and established ways of doing things and authority based on special and extraordinary powers or qualities, respectively. (D) is incorrect because all three types of authority can become institutionalized. (E) is incorrect because the question refers to political, not economic or corporate, authority.

55. **(D)** Union membership peaked in the 1950s at 25 percent of the work force and has declined steadily to about 15 percent today. (A) is wrong because corporate concentration has become even greater than a few decades ago. (B) is wrong because market forces are at least as powerful as a few decades ago. (C) is incorrect because the economic sphere is probably more important to the power elite than in the past. (E) is wrong because the industrial sector has been declining as a proportion of the economy.

56. **(B)** Caste stratification systems have both ridge boundaries between classes and ranking based on heredity. (A) and (C) are incorrect because they each only include one of the correct alternatives. (D) and (E) are incorrect because they include III (achieved statuses predominate) which is characteristic of an open or class stratification system, the opposite of a caste system. (D) also includes only one of the two correct choices.

57.   **(A)**   Intragenerational mobility refers to changes during a person's career. Chris has moved from a relatively low position in the corporation to a high position during his own career. (B) and (E) are incorrect because they refer to changes between a parent's occupational position and that of their offspring (*inter*generational mobility), and they also do not describe *mobility*, as the parent's position is relatively similar to that of their offspring. (C) is wrong because it shows no mobility, with the person moving from a carpentry position to another carpentry position. (D) is ambiguous as far as mobility is concerned, since it does not indicate anything about Nancy's occupational or economic position after quitting her nursing position.

58.   **(C)**   is correct because it is a direct statement of conflict theory's position that inequality results from the domination and exploitation of the less powerful by the more powerful. (A) is incorrect because it states the view of functionalism as to why inequality persists. (B) is wrong from all perspectives because stratification, by its nature, provides for a narrowing of the distribution of resources. (D) is incorrect because conflict theory sees the source of inequality as stemming from social structures rather than individual inadequacies. (E) is wrong because conflict theory does not claim that stratification is a rational response but rather reflects an exercise of power.

59.   **(A)**   Pluralism refers to a situation in which racial or ethnic groups live side by side but retain a distinct identity and lifestyle. (B) is wrong because it refers to the opposite process, where different groups lose their distinctive identity and lifestyle. (C) is wrong because it refers to two groups living apart from one another. (D) is incorrect; separatism refers to a minority taking steps to live apart from the majority. (E) is incorrect because it refers to a minority acquiescing to the demands of a majority.

60.   **(A)**   The amount of access to power and resources is one of the criteria that sociologists use to identify the minority status of a group. (B) and (C) are wrong because the concept of minority group does not depend on a group's relative numbers in a society. (D) is incorrect because a minority group, by definition, does not wield power. (E) is wrong because a minority may be recent immigrants but immigrants are not minorities if they are not denied access to power.

61. **(C)** Research shows that prejudice and discrimination flourish when two groups must compete for scarce resources. Research shows that (A), (B), and (E) are situations in which prejudice and discrimination tend to be low: cooperative situations, equal-status contact, and the achievement of equivalent goals. (D) is wrong because, if complete assimilation has occurred, there are no longer two separate groups, so intergroup prejudice and discrimination occur.

62. **(C)** Comparable worth refers to programs to pay the same wages for jobs that have comparable responsibilities or require comparable skills. It is intended to change situations where men get paid more for doing jobs that are not the same, but are comparable to, jobs that women do. (A) is wrong because it refers to the general ideology of gender equality and does not focus especially on income equity. (B) is wrong because sexism refers to the beliefs that justify gender inequalities. (D) is incorrect because it refers to a situation where male and female traits are not rigidly assigned to people. (E) is wrong because it refers to a situation where a minority tries to separate from a dominant group.

63. **(D)** White-collar and service workers have been growing as a proportion of the work force while blue-collar and farm workers have been declining. (D) is the only choice that includes only these two occupational categories. (A) is wrong because it includes only one of those categories. (B), (C), and (E) include one of the job categories in decline.

64. **(A)** The three core population processes identified by demographers are fertility (births), mortality (deaths), and migration (movement into or out of an area). The other choices are wrong because they include only two of these and a third which is not one of the basic demographic processes. Community (B) refers to a place where people live rather than a demographic process; fecundity (C) refers to the potential number of children that can be born, but actual fertility is the key demographic process; segregation (D) refers to the isolating of people or activities in particular parts of a city; and ecology (E) refers to the field that studies population distributions rather than an element that determines population size and distribution.

65.   **(C)**   Research shows that, as economic development (industrialization, urbanization, higher levels of education) expands, birth rates tend to decline. (A) and (D) are wrong because, when women have a choice about how many children to have, they tend to have fewer children; Family planning and gender equality give women that choice. (B) is incorrect because urbanization is a part of economic development which tends to reduce birth rates. (E) is wrong because patriarchy involves the subordination of women which is associated with less choice for women and higher birth rates.

66.   **(E)**   *Gesellschaft* is the German word used by Ferdinand Tonnies to refer to the highly impersonal and individualistic social relationships that predominate in urban life. (A) is wrong because *gemeinschaft* is the word Tonnies used to describe the opposite: the personal, more collectively oriented relationships found in small towns and rural communities. (B), (C), and (D) are terms unrelated to distinguishing between social relations in urban and rural areas: in-groups are groups people belong to and identify with; groupthink refers to a form of decision making in groups; and *verstehen* is the German word for a research methodology in sociology.

67.   **(A)**   The subway riders exhibit no interaction or group awareness. A social aggregate is a collection of people who happen to be in the same place at the same time but with no interaction or group awareness. (B), (C), and (E) are wrong because these collections of people exhibit either interaction with one another or awareness of group membership. (D) is wrong because it describes a social category (all members share a social characteristic), but all members are not in the same place at the same time.

68.   **(C)**   Primary groups are close intimate groups such as friendships or families. (A) is wrong because it is the opposite of a primary group, namely a utilitarian and impersonal group. (B) is a group to which a person doesn't belong and feels neutral or negative toward—definitely not a friendship group. (D) is wrong because there is no such group as a postindustrial group. (E) is incorrect because friendship groups are informal.

69. **(D)** A folkway is a norm that is customary and popular but not required and involves no moral overtone. (A) is wrong because mores involve required, strong rules and have moral significance. Hand-shaking does not fit this. (B) is wrong because it refers to a very strong more. (C) is incorrect because hand-shaking is not required by law. (E) is wrong because sanctions are rewards and punishments, which are not involved in the hand-shaking ritual.

70. **(A)** Sutherland's theory is based on the assumption that deviance is learned through socialization and that the looking-glass self and significant others play an important part. (B) is wrong because Merton's theory is based on the assumption of the functionalist perspective that deviance arises from anomie, a condition where the parts of society are not well integrated. (C) and (E) are wrong because those are theories of urban development rather than deviance. (D) is incorrect because it is a biological theory of deviance.

71. **(C)** An expressive crowd is one whose primary purpose and activity is the release of emotions. (A) is wrong because an acting crowd is one that takes some action toward a target, which the fans are not doing. (B) is wrong because a casual crowd is one that shows some common focus of attention but relatively little emotional expression, interaction, or organization. (D) is incorrect because a rioting crowd refers to a type of acting crowd. (E) is wrong because mass hysteria refers to an emotional reaction to some anxiety-producing event, which is not the case for the fans whose reaction is more one of joy than anxiety.

72. **(B)** Diffusion involves one group borrowing cultural items from another group. The Europeans borrowed tobacco from the New World Indians. (A) and (E) are incorrect because they both involve the creation of something new or a new use, which was not the case with tobacco. (C) is wrong because it refers to the gap between technological developments and social practices. (D) is wrong because it refers to a social movement focusing on changing a political system, which is irrelevant to the case of tobacco.

73. **(D)** Comte is considered the first to formulate the idea of a separate field of study that tried to understand society from a scientific vantage point. (A) is wrong because Durkheim is better known for his functionalist approach to topics such as religion and suicide. (B) is wrong because Parsons is a much later figure best known for his development of the

functionalist perspective. (C) is wrong because Marx was a little later than Comte and focused more on promoting political and economic change than on developing a scientific discipline. (E) is wrong because Spencer came later than Comte and built on his pioneering work.

74. **(A)** A survey could be done quickly and inexpensively over the phone or through the mail. (B) is normally used when a group is small and in a confined geographic location. (C) is wrong because it would be very expensive and time-consuming. (D) is wrong because it would also require going to many locations to collect the data. (E) is wrong because laboratory experiments normally involve bringing all the people being studied to one location.

75. **(C)** Exchange theory is based on the assumption that people seek the best outcomes for themselves by weighing benefits and costs. (A) and (E) are incorrect because they address the functionalist assumptions of interrelatedness, interdependence, and stability. (B) is wrong because it states the symbolic interactionist concern with deriving meaning and interpreting reality. (D) is wrong because it addresses the conflict theory concerns with power and domination.

76. **(C)** C. Wright Mills' power-elite theory of government contends that a small group of military, corporate, and government leaders control the fate of the United States. Although citizens believe they genuinely run the government through elected representation, in actuality, citizens have no power. (A), (B), and (D) are incorrect as Mills contends it is these groups who hold all of the power. Since a correct answer has been provided, (E) is incorrect.

77. **(B)** Polygamy refers to a form of marriage in which a member can simultaneously have more than one husband or wife. Since Mike has more than one wife, he is in a polygamous marriage. (A) Polyandry is a specific type of polygamy where a woman can have more than one husband. Since Mike has more than one wife, but Sarah and Beth do not have more than one husband, they are not in a polyandrous marriage. (C) Monogamy refers to a form of marriage where only two people are married to each other. Since there are three people in this marriage, it is not a monogamous relationship. (D) An orgy refers to sexual relations where more than two people are involved. This example is about a pattern of marriage, not sexual relations. (E) A cult refers to a small religious group, not necessarily a marital union.

78.   **(A)**   A matrilocal residence is one where, after marriage, a couple moves near the parents of the wife. Since Lorraine and Bob are moving near Lorraine's parents, their pattern of residence is characterized as matrilocal. (B) A patrilocal residence is one where a married couple move near the husband's family. Lorraine and Bob are not moving near Bob's family; therefore, their pattern of residence cannot be described as patrilocal. (C) Matrilineal refers not to a pattern of residence but a system of kinship which favors the relatives of the mother. (D) Monogamy is a type of marriage consisting of only two partners. Although Lorraine and Bob may be monogamous, this term does not describe their pattern movement near Lorraine's family. (E) Polygamy is a form of marriage where an individual can have more than one spouse. This example gives no indication that either Lorraine or Bob have another spouse.

79.   **(D)**   Tracking is the placing of students into specific curriculum groups on the basis of their perceived academic capabilities. It is a tool used for sorting and channeling students into subordinate and desirable positions in society. (A) Social mobility refers to one's ability to move from one position to another in society's stratification system. (B) Cultural capital is the social and economic advantages passed on to later generations. One's cultural capital may influence which track they are placed into, but it does not refer to the specific curriculum groups themselves. (C) Socialization is the process of learning the values, attitudes, and actions suitable for individuals who belong to a certain society. (E) is incorrect, since a correct response has been provided.

80.   **(C)**   Pierre Bourdieu's term "cultural capital" refers to the social and cultural benefits passed on to succeeding generations. For example, if you come from a home where there are cultural advantages in terms of money and education, you are likely to similarly pass those benefits on to your own children. (A) is incorrect, as it is the definition of the concept of "the looking-glass-self," not of cultural capital. (B) is incorrect. This statement refers to Mead's ideas on role-taking. (D) is incorrect as this definition corresponds to the notion of ethnocentricism, when one believes other cultures are inferior to their own. (E) refers to a subculture, not cultural capital.

81.   **(D)**   Prejudice is a negative attitude toward an entire group of people. Discrimination, on the other hand, refers to a negative action or behavior toward a group of people. In this example, Martha is refusing to hire Bill on the basis of his race, which constitutes discrimination. However, the example states that she is not prejudiced. Martha can therefore be classi-

fied as a fair-weather liberal—someone who is not prejudiced, but does discriminate. (A) and (C) are incorrect since Martha discriminated against Bill by refusing to hire him on the basis of his race. (B) is incorrect since the example claims that Martha is not prejudiced. Since a correct answer has been provided, (E) is incorrect.

82. **(C)** A caste system is a system of stratification where mobility is limited or impossible. Since Denzel can never become a toy-maker, regardless of his efforts, he is in a caste system. (A) A class system is a system of social ranking based on achieved characteristics. Someone in a class system, therefore, is mobile, and there is the possibility of moving within the stratification system. Since Denzel cannot move into a higher status position, he is not a member of a class system. (B) A colonial system is a political, cultural, and social dominance over a people by a foreign government. Denzel is a member of Santa's society and is not being controlled by a foreign power. (D) A socialist system is an economic system where the means of production and distribution are collectively owned. Nothing from this example suggests that Santa's society is socialist. (E) is incorrect since a correct answer has been provided.

83. **(B)** A meritocracy is a society where one's mobility is based on individual merit, such as hard work. Those who do not rank highly, according to this logic, must not have the values it takes to be successful. The phrase "you get what you work for" suggests that those who work hard will achieve, and those who don't will not. (A) The phrase "hanging out with bad apples will make you a bad apple" refers to deviance. The differential association theory of deviance uses this line of reasoning to explain an individual's deviant behavior through the influence of the group they associate with. This is irrelevant to the idea of meritocracy. (C) is incorrect, as this is the Marxist phrase referring to the economic system of communism. (D) is exactly the opposite of meritocracy because it suggests people cannot influence their social standing through hard work. (E) is incorrect, since a correct response has been provided.

84. **(E)** Sexual harassment, a relatively common practice, is when an occupational authority makes sexual overtures or demands on an employee. Sometimes it is overt, and other times it is very subtle. Seven out of ten women report some type of workplace sexual advancement, hints, or demands. Choices (A), (B), (C), and (D) are incorrect as they do not even approximate the actual number of women self-reporting some form of sexual harassment in the workplace.

85. **(E)** Ethnographic research on the "underclass" by Elliot Leibow and others has demonstrated that many of our previously held notions about poverty are incorrect. (A) Most welfare recipients are not able-bodied adults, but children and elderly—groups of people who are often unable to work. (B) Recent findings suggest that women on welfare have an average of 1.9 children, remarkably close to the national average. Women on welfare are not "breeding carelessly" but appear to have about the same number of children as women not on welfare. (C) and (D) are incorrect. Research by Leibow has demonstrated that people in poverty suffer from underemployment rather than unemployment. They are working, but inconsistently, often due to the nature of the job. For example, some jobs are seasonal and only employ workers sporadically throughout the year. In their constant hunt for work, these individuals almost never can rise above the poverty line.

86. **(A)** Stereotyping is a thought process where an individual thinks in terms of types and categories that are rigid and inflexible. (B) is incorrect; A selective perception is when an individual perceives only those situations which reinforce their stereotype. For example, if I hold a stereotype that all overweight people are lazy, I may only notice (selectively perceive) those instances where a person who is overweight is lazy. I fail to recognize the many overweight people who work very hard and are not lazy. (C) Scapegoating is the process of displacing blame. If the unemployment is high, for example, I may blame Mexican-American immigrants for allegedly stealing all of the good jobs. (D) Discrimination is a negative action toward a group. Thinking in terms of fixed categories is a thought process, not a behavior. Because a correct answer has been provided, (E) is incorrect.

87. **(C)** Davis and Moore contend that some jobs pay better and have more prestige due to the fact that such jobs are more necessary for the good of the society, and require greater amounts of education and training. Because these jobs require more training and education, the society must reward these extra efforts by granting more pay and prestige to these jobs. (A) is incorrect. How prestigious a job is, according to Davis and Moore, is an outcome of where a job falls. If it is a more difficult job, the society must compensate through rewards of high pay and prestige. (B) Where the job lies with respect to the means of production is unrelated to its level of prestige and pay, according to Davis and Moore. Such a statement refers more to conflict (Marxian) perspective than the functionalist perspective of Davis and Moore. (D) Physical risk of a job, per se, is generally unrelated to its positional ranking. For example, a policeman may be in a more

risky physical job; however, he has less prestige and gets paid less that an accountant whose job poses little physical risk. (E) is incorrect since a correct response has been provided.

88.   **(D)**   Discrimination refers to a negative action or behavior directed at a particular group, and a prejudice refers to the negative attitude held. (A) is incorrect because although the first answer of discrimination fits, the second response of ageism does not. Ageism is a specific type of prejudice or discrimination on the basis of one's age. Nothing from this example implies that age is the reason for the negative attitude. (B) is incorrect, as scapegoating is not necessarily an action or behavior. It may simply be where one places blame ideologically. (C) Ethnocentrism is the belief that other cultures are subordinate to one's own. Again, this term does not fit the first part of the question in that ethnocentrism is a belief, not an action or an attitude. (E) is incorrect since a correct answer has been provided.

89.   **(A)**   *Brown v. Board of Education of Topeka* was the landmark Supreme Court case that made segregation in the public school system illegal. The court ruled that "separate educational facilities are inherently unequal." Repealing "separate but equal" led to the fear, on the part of many urban whites, of infiltration of black students into predominantly white schools. (B), (C), and (D) are incorrect, as they refer to other land-mark court decisions. *Roe v. Wade* ruled that women had a legal right to an abortion. *Plessy v. Ferguson* allowed "separate but equal" facilities and public accommodation for whites and blacks in America. *Bakke v. University of California* ruled that, in Bakke's particular case, reverse discrimination had occurred in that he was a more qualified applicant than a number of minority applicants. (E) is incorrect since a correct response has been provided.

90.   **(D)**   Life span is the maximum number of years that an individual can live. This number remains unaltered because the number of years humans can live is finite. (A) Crude death rate refers to the number of deaths per 1,000 people in a given year. (B) Infant mortality rate is the number of deaths of infants under one year of age per 1,000 in a given year. (C) Life expectancy differs from life span in that while the life span is the maximum number of years humans can live, life expectancy is the average number of years an individual can expect to live under current conditions. For example, in the United States, the average life expectancy is 75 years. (E) is incorrect since a correct response has been provided.

91.   **(B)**   According to Wallerstein, World Systems Theory is a sophisticated approach to looking at global inequality. The world system, the patterns of economic and political links stretching across the globe, consists of three tiers—the core, semi-periphery, and periphery. The core countries, consisting of Germany, the United States, and Japan, are those in which modern economies originated and which have undergone industrialization. Ireland is classified by Wallerstein and his colleagues as a semi-peripheral country. Therefore choices (A), (C), and (D), all core countries, are incorrect. (E) is incorrect since a correct answer has been provided.

92.   **(A)**   Cultural association theory of deviance contends that deviance is learned through social interactions. By saying that one becomes deviant by "hanging out with the wrong crowd" implies that the individual learned deviant behaviors via social interaction with this "wrong" crowd. (B) Strain theory focuses on goals and means for achieving those goals. Individuals who deviate do so because their legitimate opportunities for success have been blocked. The phrase "hanging out with the wrong crowd" does not address the dynamics of an individual trying to achieve particular goals, but who has limited means. (C) Labeling theory focuses more on how an individual becomes labeled as deviant, in spite of the fact that another person committing the same deviant act may not become labeled. This theory does not address why some people come to commit acts, only why they become labeled as deviant. (D) Control theory focuses not on why some individuals deviate, but why they conform. The question specifically asks why an individual may deviate, not conform. (E) is incorrect, since a correct answer has been provided.

93.   **(C)**   According to Jack Gibbs's Deterrence theory, if punishments for crimes were swift, certain, and severe, individuals would be deterred from committing crimes and the crime rate would drop. By swift, he means that punishments need to immediately follow the crime. Because the current criminal justice system is heavily bureaucratized, punishments are sometimes administered long after the crime has been committed. By certain, Gibbs means that an individual committing a crime needs to know that he will undoubtedly be punished. In today's justice system, so much discretion is used that a specific punishment following a specific crime is not certain, but variable. Since Gibbs's theory makes no mention of how long-lasting the punishment is, (C) is the correct response. (A), (B), and (D) are incorrect, as they make up the crux of his theory. (E) is incorrect since a correct response has been provided.

94. **(E)** Norms are rules or standards that govern behavior. All societies encourage and enforce certain behaviors while discouraging other types. Values are a collective conception of what is deemed good or proper in a culture. Values justify norms. For example, a society may have a norm of school attendance from the ages of 5-18. The society justifies this norm through a value which places emphasis on having a highly educated and skilled population. (A) and (C) are incorrect. A role is a set of expectations for people who occupy a particular status. This differs from a norm, or a rule that governs behavior. (B) is incorrect. Norms are not used to justify a behavior, they are rules themselves. (D) is incorrect, because a more is a specific type of norm that has been institutionalized and formalized. For example, we have norms against murder and rape. The second part is additionally incorrect. A subculture is a culture within a culture. Subcultures do not justify norms.

95. **(C)** According to Cooley's notion of the "looking-glass-self," an individual's self-concept is achieved by our impressions of how others perceive us. (A) is incorrect because although parents can be very influential in shaping our self-concept, it is not only our parents, but all people, that help shape our self-concept. (B) is incorrect as the "looking-glass-self" refers to how we come to see ourselves, not how we view other people. (D) The formation of our self-concept, according to Cooley, is a social process, not a biological one. (E) is incorrect since a correct response has been provided.

96. **(A)** Aggregates are collections of people who are in the same place at the same time, but share no relationship to one another. All of the people on an escalator in a mall form such a group since they are a random collection of people who share no relationship to one another. (B) A secondary group is incorrect because people forming a secondary group share a relationship. A secondary group is made up of people who have regular contact, but are connected impersonally. (C) A social category is a collection of people who are classified together for statistical reasons on the basis of some shared characteristics, such as same race, or occupation. Since people riding on an escalator do not necessarily share common characteristics for which they are grouped together for statistical purposes, they do not form a social category. (D) A primary group is a small association of people who are bound by emotional ties, such as a family. (E) A coalition is an alliance of people toward a common goal. Nothing from this example suggests that the collection of people on the escalator at the mall are uniting around a particular goal.

97.   **(E)**   Random assignment is a technique used where individuals are placed randomly into the experimental and control groups. This technique ensures that the groups will be similar. (A) Participant observation is a research technique where the researcher collects information through direct involvement and interaction with the group. This example specifies that Lynn is doing an experiment. The participant observation method differs from the experimental method. (B) A convenience sample is a sample that is obtained conveniently. For example, a researcher may interview people whom she knows. There are no experimental and control groups in a convenience sample. (C) Reliability refers not to a method used to ensure that experimental and control groups are similar, but to the extent to which a measure provides consistent results. (D) An unobtrusive measure is one where the researcher does not get involved with those whom he is studying. It is unrelated to a technique used to ensure that groups are similar.

98.   **(D)**   G. H. Mead's "taking the role of the other" refers to the ability of people to understand another's perspective. For example, a child may learn that after coming home from work tired, his mother wants a few minutes of peace and quiet. Understanding the role of his mother, he may therefore wait before making a request. (B) "Taking the role of the other" does not involve persuasion. Instead, it is a normal stage of development in humans where they become aware of other's perspectives. (C) Mead says that during the preparatory stage of development a child learns to mimic his parents. Role playing, however, takes place during the play stage, not the preparatory stage. (E) is incorrect since a correct answer choice has been provided.

99.   **(A)**   Emile Durkheim differentiated between four types of suicide: altruistic, egoistic, anomic, and fatalistic. In altruistic suicide, an individual is overcommitted to the group to which he belongs. His moral obligation to the group is so strong that he is willing to place the welfare of the group above his own life. Since Bob is committing suicide for the good of his group, he is placing his personal welfare as secondary. (B) In egoistic suicide, the individual lacks contact and connections with the larger society. Bob does not lack connection to the society; in fact, he is too connected. (C) In anomic suicide, larger societal disorders impact the individual. Norms which once dictated behavior are now meaningless. The suicide stemming from such "normlessness" is referred to as anomic. Nothing from this example implies that the larger society has become socially disorganized. (D) Fatalistic suicide occurs when all aspects of an individual's

life are regulated to an unacceptable extent, so that the individual sees "no way out." Since a correct response is provided, (E) is incorrect.

100. **(C)** In order for her survey to have any validity and generalizability, Jane needs to administer a survey to randomly sampled respondents. Only (C) takes into consideration random sampling. (A), (B), and (D) are all examples of convenience samples. In this case, the researcher is finding the most convenient group to survey. The problem with this is that such samples lack generalizability. (E) is incorrect since a correct response has been provided.

ANSWER
SHEETS

CLEP INTRODUCTORY SOCIOLOGY

TEST 1

1. Ⓐ Ⓑ Ⓒ Ⓓ Ⓔ	34. Ⓐ Ⓑ Ⓒ Ⓓ Ⓔ	67. Ⓐ Ⓑ Ⓒ Ⓓ Ⓔ
2. Ⓐ Ⓑ Ⓒ Ⓓ Ⓔ	35. Ⓐ Ⓑ Ⓒ Ⓓ Ⓔ	68. Ⓐ Ⓑ Ⓒ Ⓓ Ⓔ
3. Ⓐ Ⓑ Ⓒ Ⓓ Ⓔ	36. Ⓐ Ⓑ Ⓒ Ⓓ Ⓔ	69. Ⓐ Ⓑ Ⓒ Ⓓ Ⓔ
4. Ⓐ Ⓑ Ⓒ Ⓓ Ⓔ	37. Ⓐ Ⓑ Ⓒ Ⓓ Ⓔ	70. Ⓐ Ⓑ Ⓒ Ⓓ Ⓔ
5. Ⓐ Ⓑ Ⓒ Ⓓ Ⓔ	38. Ⓐ Ⓑ Ⓒ Ⓓ Ⓔ	71. Ⓐ Ⓑ Ⓒ Ⓓ Ⓔ
6. Ⓐ Ⓑ Ⓒ Ⓓ Ⓔ	39. Ⓐ Ⓑ Ⓒ Ⓓ Ⓔ	72. Ⓐ Ⓑ Ⓒ Ⓓ Ⓔ
7. Ⓐ Ⓑ Ⓒ Ⓓ Ⓔ	40. Ⓐ Ⓑ Ⓒ Ⓓ Ⓔ	73. Ⓐ Ⓑ Ⓒ Ⓓ Ⓔ
8. Ⓐ Ⓑ Ⓒ Ⓓ Ⓔ	41. Ⓐ Ⓑ Ⓒ Ⓓ Ⓔ	74. Ⓐ Ⓑ Ⓒ Ⓓ Ⓔ
9. Ⓐ Ⓑ Ⓒ Ⓓ Ⓔ	42. Ⓐ Ⓑ Ⓒ Ⓓ Ⓔ	75. Ⓐ Ⓑ Ⓒ Ⓓ Ⓔ
10. Ⓐ Ⓑ Ⓒ Ⓓ Ⓔ	43. Ⓐ Ⓑ Ⓒ Ⓓ Ⓔ	76. Ⓐ Ⓑ Ⓒ Ⓓ Ⓔ
11. Ⓐ Ⓑ Ⓒ Ⓓ Ⓔ	44. Ⓐ Ⓑ Ⓒ Ⓓ Ⓔ	77. Ⓐ Ⓑ Ⓒ Ⓓ Ⓔ
12. Ⓐ Ⓑ Ⓒ Ⓓ Ⓔ	45. Ⓐ Ⓑ Ⓒ Ⓓ Ⓔ	78. Ⓐ Ⓑ Ⓒ Ⓓ Ⓔ
13. Ⓐ Ⓑ Ⓒ Ⓓ Ⓔ	46. Ⓐ Ⓑ Ⓒ Ⓓ Ⓔ	79. Ⓐ Ⓑ Ⓒ Ⓓ Ⓔ
14. Ⓐ Ⓑ Ⓒ Ⓓ Ⓔ	47. Ⓐ Ⓑ Ⓒ Ⓓ Ⓔ	80. Ⓐ Ⓑ Ⓒ Ⓓ Ⓔ
15. Ⓐ Ⓑ Ⓒ Ⓓ Ⓔ	48. Ⓐ Ⓑ Ⓒ Ⓓ Ⓔ	81. Ⓐ Ⓑ Ⓒ Ⓓ Ⓔ
16. Ⓐ Ⓑ Ⓒ Ⓓ Ⓔ	49. Ⓐ Ⓑ Ⓒ Ⓓ Ⓔ	82. Ⓐ Ⓑ Ⓒ Ⓓ Ⓔ
17. Ⓐ Ⓑ Ⓒ Ⓓ Ⓔ	50. Ⓐ Ⓑ Ⓒ Ⓓ Ⓔ	83. Ⓐ Ⓑ Ⓒ Ⓓ Ⓔ
18. Ⓐ Ⓑ Ⓒ Ⓓ Ⓔ	51. Ⓐ Ⓑ Ⓒ Ⓓ Ⓔ	84. Ⓐ Ⓑ Ⓒ Ⓓ Ⓔ
19. Ⓐ Ⓑ Ⓒ Ⓓ Ⓔ	52. Ⓐ Ⓑ Ⓒ Ⓓ Ⓔ	85. Ⓐ Ⓑ Ⓒ Ⓓ Ⓔ
20. Ⓐ Ⓑ Ⓒ Ⓓ Ⓔ	53. Ⓐ Ⓑ Ⓒ Ⓓ Ⓔ	86. Ⓐ Ⓑ Ⓒ Ⓓ Ⓔ
21. Ⓐ Ⓑ Ⓒ Ⓓ Ⓔ	54. Ⓐ Ⓑ Ⓒ Ⓓ Ⓔ	87. Ⓐ Ⓑ Ⓒ Ⓓ Ⓔ
22. Ⓐ Ⓑ Ⓒ Ⓓ Ⓔ	55. Ⓐ Ⓑ Ⓒ Ⓓ Ⓔ	88. Ⓐ Ⓑ Ⓒ Ⓓ Ⓔ
23. Ⓐ Ⓑ Ⓒ Ⓓ Ⓔ	56. Ⓐ Ⓑ Ⓒ Ⓓ Ⓔ	89. Ⓐ Ⓑ Ⓒ Ⓓ Ⓔ
24. Ⓐ Ⓑ Ⓒ Ⓓ Ⓔ	57. Ⓐ Ⓑ Ⓒ Ⓓ Ⓔ	90. Ⓐ Ⓑ Ⓒ Ⓓ Ⓔ
25. Ⓐ Ⓑ Ⓒ Ⓓ Ⓔ	58. Ⓐ Ⓑ Ⓒ Ⓓ Ⓔ	91. Ⓐ Ⓑ Ⓒ Ⓓ Ⓔ
26. Ⓐ Ⓑ Ⓒ Ⓓ Ⓔ	59. Ⓐ Ⓑ Ⓒ Ⓓ Ⓔ	92. Ⓐ Ⓑ Ⓒ Ⓓ Ⓔ
27. Ⓐ Ⓑ Ⓒ Ⓓ Ⓔ	60. Ⓐ Ⓑ Ⓒ Ⓓ Ⓔ	93. Ⓐ Ⓑ Ⓒ Ⓓ Ⓔ
28. Ⓐ Ⓑ Ⓒ Ⓓ Ⓔ	61. Ⓐ Ⓑ Ⓒ Ⓓ Ⓔ	94. Ⓐ Ⓑ Ⓒ Ⓓ Ⓔ
29. Ⓐ Ⓑ Ⓒ Ⓓ Ⓔ	62. Ⓐ Ⓑ Ⓒ Ⓓ Ⓔ	95. Ⓐ Ⓑ Ⓒ Ⓓ Ⓔ
30. Ⓐ Ⓑ Ⓒ Ⓓ Ⓔ	63. Ⓐ Ⓑ Ⓒ Ⓓ Ⓔ	96. Ⓐ Ⓑ Ⓒ Ⓓ Ⓔ
31. Ⓐ Ⓑ Ⓒ Ⓓ Ⓔ	64. Ⓐ Ⓑ Ⓒ Ⓓ Ⓔ	97. Ⓐ Ⓑ Ⓒ Ⓓ Ⓔ
32. Ⓐ Ⓑ Ⓒ Ⓓ Ⓔ	65. Ⓐ Ⓑ Ⓒ Ⓓ Ⓔ	98. Ⓐ Ⓑ Ⓒ Ⓓ Ⓔ
33. Ⓐ Ⓑ Ⓒ Ⓓ Ⓔ	66. Ⓐ Ⓑ Ⓒ Ⓓ Ⓔ	99. Ⓐ Ⓑ Ⓒ Ⓓ Ⓔ
		100. Ⓐ Ⓑ Ⓒ Ⓓ Ⓔ

CLEP INTRODUCTORY SOCIOLOGY

TEST 2

1. Ⓐ Ⓑ Ⓒ Ⓓ Ⓔ
2. Ⓐ Ⓑ Ⓒ Ⓓ Ⓔ
3. Ⓐ Ⓑ Ⓒ Ⓓ Ⓔ
4. Ⓐ Ⓑ Ⓒ Ⓓ Ⓔ
5. Ⓐ Ⓑ Ⓒ Ⓓ Ⓔ
6. Ⓐ Ⓑ Ⓒ Ⓓ Ⓔ
7. Ⓐ Ⓑ Ⓒ Ⓓ Ⓔ
8. Ⓐ Ⓑ Ⓒ Ⓓ Ⓔ
9. Ⓐ Ⓑ Ⓒ Ⓓ Ⓔ
10. Ⓐ Ⓑ Ⓒ Ⓓ Ⓔ
11. Ⓐ Ⓑ Ⓒ Ⓓ Ⓔ
12. Ⓐ Ⓑ Ⓒ Ⓓ Ⓔ
13. Ⓐ Ⓑ Ⓒ Ⓓ Ⓔ
14. Ⓐ Ⓑ Ⓒ Ⓓ Ⓔ
15. Ⓐ Ⓑ Ⓒ Ⓓ Ⓔ
16. Ⓐ Ⓑ Ⓒ Ⓓ Ⓔ
17. Ⓐ Ⓑ Ⓒ Ⓓ Ⓔ
18. Ⓐ Ⓑ Ⓒ Ⓓ Ⓔ
19. Ⓐ Ⓑ Ⓒ Ⓓ Ⓔ
20. Ⓐ Ⓑ Ⓒ Ⓓ Ⓔ
21. Ⓐ Ⓑ Ⓒ Ⓓ Ⓔ
22. Ⓐ Ⓑ Ⓒ Ⓓ Ⓔ
23. Ⓐ Ⓑ Ⓒ Ⓓ Ⓔ
24. Ⓐ Ⓑ Ⓒ Ⓓ Ⓔ
25. Ⓐ Ⓑ Ⓒ Ⓓ Ⓔ
26. Ⓐ Ⓑ Ⓒ Ⓓ Ⓔ
27. Ⓐ Ⓑ Ⓒ Ⓓ Ⓔ
28. Ⓐ Ⓑ Ⓒ Ⓓ Ⓔ
29. Ⓐ Ⓑ Ⓒ Ⓓ Ⓔ
30. Ⓐ Ⓑ Ⓒ Ⓓ Ⓔ
31. Ⓐ Ⓑ Ⓒ Ⓓ Ⓔ
32. Ⓐ Ⓑ Ⓒ Ⓓ Ⓔ
33. Ⓐ Ⓑ Ⓒ Ⓓ Ⓔ

34. Ⓐ Ⓑ Ⓒ Ⓓ Ⓔ
35. Ⓐ Ⓑ Ⓒ Ⓓ Ⓔ
36. Ⓐ Ⓑ Ⓒ Ⓓ Ⓔ
37. Ⓐ Ⓑ Ⓒ Ⓓ Ⓔ
38. Ⓐ Ⓑ Ⓒ Ⓓ Ⓔ
39. Ⓐ Ⓑ Ⓒ Ⓓ Ⓔ
40. Ⓐ Ⓑ Ⓒ Ⓓ Ⓔ
41. Ⓐ Ⓑ Ⓒ Ⓓ Ⓔ
42. Ⓐ Ⓑ Ⓒ Ⓓ Ⓔ
43. Ⓐ Ⓑ Ⓒ Ⓓ Ⓔ
44. Ⓐ Ⓑ Ⓒ Ⓓ Ⓔ
45. Ⓐ Ⓑ Ⓒ Ⓓ Ⓔ
46. Ⓐ Ⓑ Ⓒ Ⓓ Ⓔ
47. Ⓐ Ⓑ Ⓒ Ⓓ Ⓔ
48. Ⓐ Ⓑ Ⓒ Ⓓ Ⓔ
49. Ⓐ Ⓑ Ⓒ Ⓓ Ⓔ
50. Ⓐ Ⓑ Ⓒ Ⓓ Ⓔ
51. Ⓐ Ⓑ Ⓒ Ⓓ Ⓔ
52. Ⓐ Ⓑ Ⓒ Ⓓ Ⓔ
53. Ⓐ Ⓑ Ⓒ Ⓓ Ⓔ
54. Ⓐ Ⓑ Ⓒ Ⓓ Ⓔ
55. Ⓐ Ⓑ Ⓒ Ⓓ Ⓔ
56. Ⓐ Ⓑ Ⓒ Ⓓ Ⓔ
57. Ⓐ Ⓑ Ⓒ Ⓓ Ⓔ
58. Ⓐ Ⓑ Ⓒ Ⓓ Ⓔ
59. Ⓐ Ⓑ Ⓒ Ⓓ Ⓔ
60. Ⓐ Ⓑ Ⓒ Ⓓ Ⓔ
61. Ⓐ Ⓑ Ⓒ Ⓓ Ⓔ
62. Ⓐ Ⓑ Ⓒ Ⓓ Ⓔ
63. Ⓐ Ⓑ Ⓒ Ⓓ Ⓔ
64. Ⓐ Ⓑ Ⓒ Ⓓ Ⓔ
65. Ⓐ Ⓑ Ⓒ Ⓓ Ⓔ
66. Ⓐ Ⓑ Ⓒ Ⓓ Ⓔ

67. Ⓐ Ⓑ Ⓒ Ⓓ Ⓔ
68. Ⓐ Ⓑ Ⓒ Ⓓ Ⓔ
69. Ⓐ Ⓑ Ⓒ Ⓓ Ⓔ
70. Ⓐ Ⓑ Ⓒ Ⓓ Ⓔ
71. Ⓐ Ⓑ Ⓒ Ⓓ Ⓔ
72. Ⓐ Ⓑ Ⓒ Ⓓ Ⓔ
73. Ⓐ Ⓑ Ⓒ Ⓓ Ⓔ
74. Ⓐ Ⓑ Ⓒ Ⓓ Ⓔ
75. Ⓐ Ⓑ Ⓒ Ⓓ Ⓔ
76. Ⓐ Ⓑ Ⓒ Ⓓ Ⓔ
77. Ⓐ Ⓑ Ⓒ Ⓓ Ⓔ
78. Ⓐ Ⓑ Ⓒ Ⓓ Ⓔ
79. Ⓐ Ⓑ Ⓒ Ⓓ Ⓔ
80. Ⓐ Ⓑ Ⓒ Ⓓ Ⓔ
81. Ⓐ Ⓑ Ⓒ Ⓓ Ⓔ
82. Ⓐ Ⓑ Ⓒ Ⓓ Ⓔ
83. Ⓐ Ⓑ Ⓒ Ⓓ Ⓔ
84. Ⓐ Ⓑ Ⓒ Ⓓ Ⓔ
85. Ⓐ Ⓑ Ⓒ Ⓓ Ⓔ
86. Ⓐ Ⓑ Ⓒ Ⓓ Ⓔ
87. Ⓐ Ⓑ Ⓒ Ⓓ Ⓔ
88. Ⓐ Ⓑ Ⓒ Ⓓ Ⓔ
89. Ⓐ Ⓑ Ⓒ Ⓓ Ⓔ
90. Ⓐ Ⓑ Ⓒ Ⓓ Ⓔ
91. Ⓐ Ⓑ Ⓒ Ⓓ Ⓔ
92. Ⓐ Ⓑ Ⓒ Ⓓ Ⓔ
93. Ⓐ Ⓑ Ⓒ Ⓓ Ⓔ
94. Ⓐ Ⓑ Ⓒ Ⓓ Ⓔ
95. Ⓐ Ⓑ Ⓒ Ⓓ Ⓔ
96. Ⓐ Ⓑ Ⓒ Ⓓ Ⓔ
97. Ⓐ Ⓑ Ⓒ Ⓓ Ⓔ
98. Ⓐ Ⓑ Ⓒ Ⓓ Ⓔ
99. Ⓐ Ⓑ Ⓒ Ⓓ Ⓔ
100. Ⓐ Ⓑ Ⓒ Ⓓ Ⓔ

CLEP INTRODUCTORY SOCIOLOGY

TEST 3

1. Ⓐ Ⓑ Ⓒ Ⓓ Ⓔ	34. Ⓐ Ⓑ Ⓒ Ⓓ Ⓔ	67. Ⓐ Ⓑ Ⓒ Ⓓ Ⓔ
2. Ⓐ Ⓑ Ⓒ Ⓓ Ⓔ	35. Ⓐ Ⓑ Ⓒ Ⓓ Ⓔ	68. Ⓐ Ⓑ Ⓒ Ⓓ Ⓔ
3. Ⓐ Ⓑ Ⓒ Ⓓ Ⓔ	36. Ⓐ Ⓑ Ⓒ Ⓓ Ⓔ	69. Ⓐ Ⓑ Ⓒ Ⓓ Ⓔ
4. Ⓐ Ⓑ Ⓒ Ⓓ Ⓔ	37. Ⓐ Ⓑ Ⓒ Ⓓ Ⓔ	70. Ⓐ Ⓑ Ⓒ Ⓓ Ⓔ
5. Ⓐ Ⓑ Ⓒ Ⓓ Ⓔ	38. Ⓐ Ⓑ Ⓒ Ⓓ Ⓔ	71. Ⓐ Ⓑ Ⓒ Ⓓ Ⓔ
6. Ⓐ Ⓑ Ⓒ Ⓓ Ⓔ	39. Ⓐ Ⓑ Ⓒ Ⓓ Ⓔ	72. Ⓐ Ⓑ Ⓒ Ⓓ Ⓔ
7. Ⓐ Ⓑ Ⓒ Ⓓ Ⓔ	40. Ⓐ Ⓑ Ⓒ Ⓓ Ⓔ	73. Ⓐ Ⓑ Ⓒ Ⓓ Ⓔ
8. Ⓐ Ⓑ Ⓒ Ⓓ Ⓔ	41. Ⓐ Ⓑ Ⓒ Ⓓ Ⓔ	74. Ⓐ Ⓑ Ⓒ Ⓓ Ⓔ
9. Ⓐ Ⓑ Ⓒ Ⓓ Ⓔ	42. Ⓐ Ⓑ Ⓒ Ⓓ Ⓔ	75. Ⓐ Ⓑ Ⓒ Ⓓ Ⓔ
10. Ⓐ Ⓑ Ⓒ Ⓓ Ⓔ	43. Ⓐ Ⓑ Ⓒ Ⓓ Ⓔ	76. Ⓐ Ⓑ Ⓒ Ⓓ Ⓔ
11. Ⓐ Ⓑ Ⓒ Ⓓ Ⓔ	44. Ⓐ Ⓑ Ⓒ Ⓓ Ⓔ	77. Ⓐ Ⓑ Ⓒ Ⓓ Ⓔ
12. Ⓐ Ⓑ Ⓒ Ⓓ Ⓔ	45. Ⓐ Ⓑ Ⓒ Ⓓ Ⓔ	78. Ⓐ Ⓑ Ⓒ Ⓓ Ⓔ
13. Ⓐ Ⓑ Ⓒ Ⓓ Ⓔ	46. Ⓐ Ⓑ Ⓒ Ⓓ Ⓔ	79. Ⓐ Ⓑ Ⓒ Ⓓ Ⓔ
14. Ⓐ Ⓑ Ⓒ Ⓓ Ⓔ	47. Ⓐ Ⓑ Ⓒ Ⓓ Ⓔ	80. Ⓐ Ⓑ Ⓒ Ⓓ Ⓔ
15. Ⓐ Ⓑ Ⓒ Ⓓ Ⓔ	48. Ⓐ Ⓑ Ⓒ Ⓓ Ⓔ	81. Ⓐ Ⓑ Ⓒ Ⓓ Ⓔ
16. Ⓐ Ⓑ Ⓒ Ⓓ Ⓔ	49. Ⓐ Ⓑ Ⓒ Ⓓ Ⓔ	82. Ⓐ Ⓑ Ⓒ Ⓓ Ⓔ
17. Ⓐ Ⓑ Ⓒ Ⓓ Ⓔ	50. Ⓐ Ⓑ Ⓒ Ⓓ Ⓔ	83. Ⓐ Ⓑ Ⓒ Ⓓ Ⓔ
18. Ⓐ Ⓑ Ⓒ Ⓓ Ⓔ	51. Ⓐ Ⓑ Ⓒ Ⓓ Ⓔ	84. Ⓐ Ⓑ Ⓒ Ⓓ Ⓔ
19. Ⓐ Ⓑ Ⓒ Ⓓ Ⓔ	52. Ⓐ Ⓑ Ⓒ Ⓓ Ⓔ	85. Ⓐ Ⓑ Ⓒ Ⓓ Ⓔ
20. Ⓐ Ⓑ Ⓒ Ⓓ Ⓔ	53. Ⓐ Ⓑ Ⓒ Ⓓ Ⓔ	86. Ⓐ Ⓑ Ⓒ Ⓓ Ⓔ
21. Ⓐ Ⓑ Ⓒ Ⓓ Ⓔ	54. Ⓐ Ⓑ Ⓒ Ⓓ Ⓔ	87. Ⓐ Ⓑ Ⓒ Ⓓ Ⓔ
22. Ⓐ Ⓑ Ⓒ Ⓓ Ⓔ	55. Ⓐ Ⓑ Ⓒ Ⓓ Ⓔ	88. Ⓐ Ⓑ Ⓒ Ⓓ Ⓔ
23. Ⓐ Ⓑ Ⓒ Ⓓ Ⓔ	56. Ⓐ Ⓑ Ⓒ Ⓓ Ⓔ	89. Ⓐ Ⓑ Ⓒ Ⓓ Ⓔ
24. Ⓐ Ⓑ Ⓒ Ⓓ Ⓔ	57. Ⓐ Ⓑ Ⓒ Ⓓ Ⓔ	90. Ⓐ Ⓑ Ⓒ Ⓓ Ⓔ
25. Ⓐ Ⓑ Ⓒ Ⓓ Ⓔ	58. Ⓐ Ⓑ Ⓒ Ⓓ Ⓔ	91. Ⓐ Ⓑ Ⓒ Ⓓ Ⓔ
26. Ⓐ Ⓑ Ⓒ Ⓓ Ⓔ	59. Ⓐ Ⓑ Ⓒ Ⓓ Ⓔ	92. Ⓐ Ⓑ Ⓒ Ⓓ Ⓔ
27. Ⓐ Ⓑ Ⓒ Ⓓ Ⓔ	60. Ⓐ Ⓑ Ⓒ Ⓓ Ⓔ	93. Ⓐ Ⓑ Ⓒ Ⓓ Ⓔ
28. Ⓐ Ⓑ Ⓒ Ⓓ Ⓔ	61. Ⓐ Ⓑ Ⓒ Ⓓ Ⓔ	94. Ⓐ Ⓑ Ⓒ Ⓓ Ⓔ
29. Ⓐ Ⓑ Ⓒ Ⓓ Ⓔ	62. Ⓐ Ⓑ Ⓒ Ⓓ Ⓔ	95. Ⓐ Ⓑ Ⓒ Ⓓ Ⓔ
30. Ⓐ Ⓑ Ⓒ Ⓓ Ⓔ	63. Ⓐ Ⓑ Ⓒ Ⓓ Ⓔ	96. Ⓐ Ⓑ Ⓒ Ⓓ Ⓔ
31. Ⓐ Ⓑ Ⓒ Ⓓ Ⓔ	64. Ⓐ Ⓑ Ⓒ Ⓓ Ⓔ	97. Ⓐ Ⓑ Ⓒ Ⓓ Ⓔ
32. Ⓐ Ⓑ Ⓒ Ⓓ Ⓔ	65. Ⓐ Ⓑ Ⓒ Ⓓ Ⓔ	98. Ⓐ Ⓑ Ⓒ Ⓓ Ⓔ
33. Ⓐ Ⓑ Ⓒ Ⓓ Ⓔ	66. Ⓐ Ⓑ Ⓒ Ⓓ Ⓔ	99. Ⓐ Ⓑ Ⓒ Ⓓ Ⓔ
		100. Ⓐ Ⓑ Ⓒ Ⓓ Ⓔ

ABOUT RESEARCH & EDUCATION ASSOCIATION

Founded in 1959, Research & Education Association (REA) is dedicated to publishing the finest and most effective educational materials—including software, study guides, and test preps—for students in middle school, high school, college, graduate school, and beyond.

REA's Test Preparation series includes books and software for all academic levels in almost all disciplines. Research & Education Association publishes test preps for students who have not yet entered high school, as well as high school students preparing to enter college. Students from countries around the world seeking to attend college in the United States will find the assistance they need in REA's publications. For college students seeking advanced degrees, REA publishes test preps for many major graduate school admission examinations in a wide variety of disciplines, including engineering, law, and medicine. Students at every level, in every field, with every ambition can find what they are looking for among REA's publications.

REA presents tests that accurately depict the official exams in both degree of difficulty and types of questions. REA's practice tests are always based upon the most recently administered exams, and include every type of question that can be expected on the actual exams.

REA's publications and educational materials are highly regarded and continually receive an unprecedented amount of praise from professionals, instructors, librarians, parents, and students. Our authors are as diverse as the fields represented in the books we publish. They are well known in their respective disciplines and serve on the faculties of prestigious high schools, colleges, and universities throughout the United States and Canada.

Today REA's wide-ranging catalog is a leading resource for teachers, students, and professionals.

We invite you to visit us at *www.rea.com* to find out how "REA is making the world smarter."

ACKNOWLEDGMENTS

In addition to our authors, we would like to thank Larry B. Kling, Vice President, Editorial, for his overall direction; Pam Weston, Vice President, Publishing, for setting the quality standards for production integrity and managing the publication to completion; Diane Goldschmidt and Anne Winthrop Esposito, Senior Editors, for coordinating revisions; Christine Saul, Senior Graphic Designer, for designing the cover; and Rachel DiMatteo, Graphic Designer, for typesetting revisions.

REA'S
PROBLEM
SOLVERS®

The PROBLEM SOLVERS® are comprehensive supplemental textbooks designed to save time in finding solutions to problems. Each PROBLEM SOLVER® is the first of its kind ever produced in its field. It is the product of a massive effort to illustrate almost any imaginable problem in exceptional depth, detail, and clarity. Each problem is worked out in detail with a step-by-step solution, and the problems are arranged in order of complexity from elementary to advanced. Each book is fully indexed for locating problems rapidly.

Accounting	Genetics
Advanced Calculus	Geometry
Algebra & Trigonometry	Linear Algebra
Automatic Control Systems/Robotics	Mechanics
Biology	Numerical Analysis
Business, Accounting & Finance	Operations Research
Calculus	Organic Chemistry
Chemistry	Physics
Differential Equations	Pre-Calculus
Economics	Probability
Electrical Machines	Psychology
Electric Circuits	Statistics
Electromagnetics	Technical Design Graphics
Electronics	Thermodynamics
Finite & Discrete Math	Topology
Fluid Mechanics/Dynamics	Transport Phenomena

*If you would like more information about any of these books,
complete the coupon below and return it to us or visit your local bookstore.*

Research & Education Association
61 Ethel Road W., Piscataway, NJ 08854
Phone: (732) 819-8880   **website: www.rea.com**

Please send me more information about your Problem Solver® books.

Name _____

Address _____

City _____ State _____ Zip _____

REA's Test Prep Books Are The Best!

(a sample of the <u>hundreds of letters</u> REA receives each year)

" I am writing to congratulate you on preparing an exceptional study guide. In five years of teaching this course I have never encountered a more thorough, comprehensive, concise and realistic preparation for this examination. "

Teacher, Davie, FL

" I have found your publications, *The Best Test Preparation...*, to be exactly that. "

Teacher, Aptos, CA

" I used your *CLEP Introductory Sociology* book and rank it 99% — thank you! "

Student, Jerusalem, Israel

" Your *GMAT* book greatly helped me on the test. Thank you. "

Student, Oxford, OH

" I recently got the *French SAT II* Exam book from REA. I congratulate you on first-rate French practice tests. "

Instructor, Los Angeles, CA

" Your *AP English Literature and Composition* book is most impressive. "

Student, Montgomery, AL

" The REA *LSAT* Test Preparation guide is a winner! "

Instructor, Spartanburg, SC

(more on front page)